SELECTED
DOCUMENTS IN
IRISH
HISTORY

SELECTED DOCUMENTS IN IRISH HISTORY

JOSEF L. ALTHOLZ

M.E.Sharpe
Armonk, New York
London, England

Library of Congress Cataloging-in-Publication Data

Selected documents in Irish history / [compiled by] Josef L. Altholz.
    p. cm.
  ISBN 0-7656-0541-4 (hardcover : alk. paper)
  ISBN 0-7656-0542-2 (pbk. : alk. paper)
    1. Ireland—History—Sources. I. Altholz, Josef L., 1933–
DA905 .S35 2000
941.5—dc21   99-046033
  CIP

Printed in the United States of America

The paper used in this publication meets the minimum requirements of
American National Standard for Information Sciences
Permanence of Paper for Printed Library Materials,
ANSI Z 39.48-1984.

BM (c) 10   9   8   7   6   5   4   3   2
BM (p) 10   9   8   7   6   5   4   3

Contents

Preface

This book is designed as a collection of readings to accompany the growing number of courses in Irish history being taught in North America. We have at least two textbooks suitable for American college students, but there is a lack of supplementary materials other than films and videos. The need for a book of readings has been borne in on me by two decades of teaching Irish history, and the need increases especially as I plan to expand the course from one quarter to one semester. One would like to have class discussions, but this is a chancy thing in a subject such as Irish history, to which nearly every student brings opinions but few bring knowledge. Discussion can be controlled if focused on specific texts, which are themselves worthy of careful study.

I am solely responsible for the selection of documents, except for some happy suggestions from Professor Emmet Larkin, the dean of Irish history in America, and from Professor Karl S. Bottigheimer, the author of the textbook *Ireland and the Irish*. I have kept my introductory comments as brief as possible, since I expect these documents to be used in conjunction with a textbook. I have preferred to use original printed sources where possible, even retaining the original spelling and punctuation, which should not deter but rather fascinate American readers. Otherwise, I follow the collections on which I have drawn. I have condensed and edited in order to keep this volume as short and inexpensive as possible; but if I have erred, it has been on the side of inclusiveness and representativeness.

SELECTED
DOCUMENTS IN
IRISH
HISTORY

1

St. Patrick: *Confessio*

St. Patrick undoubtedly led an effective mission in Ireland from the 430s; legend credits him with converting the whole island. The historical facts are uncertain, and perhaps irrelevant: in Ireland, myth often makes history. Patrick's own *Confessio* is just what that word meant in the Middle Ages: not so much an autobiography as a confession of faith, an apology or self-justification, ultimately a cry of the heart.

Reproduced by kind permission from ARTHURIAN PERIOD SOURCES (General Editor John Morris), volume 9 *St. Patrick* (edited and translated by A.B.E. Hood), published in 1978 by Phillimore & Co., Ltd., Shopwyke Manor Barn, Chichester, West Sussex, England.

1. I, Patrick, a sinner, quite uncultivated and the least of all the faithful and utterly despicable to many, had as my father the deacon Calpornius, son of the late Potitus, a priest, who belonged to the town of Bannavem Taburniae; he had a small estate nearby, and it was there that I was taken captive. I was then about sixteen years old. I did not know the true God and I was taken into captivity in Ireland with so many thousands; and we deserved it, because we drew away from God and did not keep His commandments and did not obey our priests who kept reminding us of our salvation; and the Lord brought on us the fury of His anger and scattered us among many peoples even to the

ends of the earth, where now I in my insignificance find myself among foreigners.

2. And there the Lord opened up my awareness of my unbelief, so that I might, however late, remember my faults and turn with all my heart to the Lord my God, who had regard for my lowly estate and took pity on my youth and ignorance. . . .

16. But after I reached Ireland, well, I pastured the flocks every day and I used to pray many times a day; more and more did my love of God and my fear of Him increase, and my faith grew and my spirit was stirred, and as a result I would say up to a hundred prayers in one day, and almost as many at night; I would even stay in the forests and on the mountain and would wake to pray before dawn in all weathers, snow, frost, rain; and I felt no harm and there was no listlessness in me—as I now realise, it was because the Spirit was fervent within me.

17. And it was in fact there that one night while asleep I heard a voice saying to me: 'You do well to fast, since you will soon be going to your home country;' and again, very shortly after, I heard this prophecy: 'See, your ship is ready.' And it was not near at hand but was perhaps two hundred miles away, and I had never been there and did not know a living soul there. And I soon ran away and abandoned the man with whom I had been for six years, and I came in God's strength, for He granted me a successful journey and I had nothing to fear, till I reached that ship. . . .

23. And again a few years later I was in Britain with my kinsfolk, and they welcomed me as a son and asked me earnestly not to go off anywhere and leave them this time, after the great tribulations which I had been through. And it was there that I saw one night in a vision a man coming as it were from Ireland (his name was Victoricus), with countless letters, and he gave me one of them, and I read the heading of the letter, 'The Voice

of the Irish,' and as I read these opening words aloud, I imagined at that very instant that I heard the voice of those who were beside the forest of Foclut which is near the western sea; and thus they cried, as though with one voice: 'We beg you, holy boy, to come and walk again among us,' and I was stung with remorse in my heart and could not read on, and so I awoke. Thanks be to God, that after so many years the Lord bestowed on them according to their cry. . . .

41. And how has it lately come about in Ireland that those who never had any knowledge of God but up till now always worshipped idols and abominations are now called the people of the Lord and the sons of God, and sons and daughters of Irish underkings are seen to be monks and virgins of Christ?. . . .

58. And so may God never allow me to be separated from His people which He has won in the ends of the earth. I pray to God to give me perseverance and to deign to grant that I prove a faithful witness to Him until I pass on, for my God's sake. . . .

62. But I beg those who believe in and fear God, whoever deigns to look at or receive this document which the unlearned sinner Patrick drew up in Ireland, that no-one should ever say that if I have achieved anything, however trivial, or may have shown the way according to God's good pleasure, it was my ignorance at work, but consider and accept as the undeniable truth that it would have been God's gift. And this is my declaration before I die.

2

Muirchu's Life of St. Patrick

Muirchu's life of St. Patrick, written two centuries later, is the oldest to survive. It displays a characteristic mixture of the factual and the miraculous.

Reproduced by kind permission from ARTHURIAN PERIOD SOURCES (General Editor, John Morris), volume 9 *St. Patrick* (edited and translated by A.B.E. Hood), published in 1978 by Phillimore & Co., Ltd., Shopwyke Manor Barn, Chichester, West Sussex, England.

These few items concerning St. Patrick's experience and miraculous powers were written down by Muirchu maccu Machtheni under the direction of Aed, bishop of the town of Sletty.

1. Patrick, who was also called Sochet, was of British nationality, born in Britain, the son of the deacon Calpurnius, whose father, as Patrick himself says, was the priest Potitus, who came from the town of Bannavem Taburniae, not far from our sea; we have discovered for certain and beyond any doubt that this township is Ventre; and the mother who bore him was named Concessa.

At the age of sixteen the boy, with others, was captured and brought to this island of barbarians and was kept as a slave in the household of a certain cruel pagan king. He spent six years in captivity, in accordance with the Jewish custom, in fear and trembling before God, as the psalmist says (*Psalms 54, 6*), and in many vigils and prayers. He used to pray a hundred times a day and a hundred times a night, gladly giving to God what is due to God and to Caesar what is due to Caesar and beginning to fear God and to love the Lord Almighty; for up to that time he had no knowledge of the true God, but at this point the Spirit became fervent within him.

After many hardships there, after enduring hunger and thirst, cold and nakedness, after pasturing flocks, after visits from Victoricus, an angel sent to him by God, after great miracles known to almost everyone, after divine prophecies (of which I shall give just one or two examples: 'You do well to fast, since you will soon be going to your home country,' and again: 'See, your ship is ready,' though it was not near at hand but was perhaps two hundred miles away, where he had never been to)— after all these experiences, as we have said, which can hardly be counted by anyone, in the twenty-third year of his life he left the earthly, pagan king and his works, received the heavenly, eternal God and now sailed for Britain by God's command and accompanied by the Holy Spirit in the ship which lay ready for him; with him were barbarian strangers and pagans who worshipped many false gods. . . .

8. And so, when a suitable opportunity so directed, with God's help to accompany him he set out on the journey which he had already begun, to the work for which he had long been prepared—the work, that is, of the Gospel. And Germanus sent an older man with him, namely the priest Segitius, so that Patrick would have a witness and companion, since he had not yet been consecrated to the rank of bishop by the holy lord Germanus. For they were well aware that Palladius, the archdeacon of Pope Celestine, the bishop of the city of Rome who then held the

apostolic see as forty-fifth in line from St. Peter the apostle, that this Palladius had been consecrated and sent to convert his island, lying as it does in frozen wintriness. But God prevented him, because no one can receive anything from this earth unless it has been given him from heaven. For these wild, uncivilised people did not take kindly to his teaching, nor did he himself want to spend time in a land which was not his own; he returned to him who sent him. But on his return journey from here, after making the first sea crossing and proceeding by land, he died in the land of the British.

9. And so, when the word came of the death of St. Palladius in Britain, since Palladius' disciples, Augustine, Benedict and the others, returned to Ebmoria with the news of his death, Patrick and his companions turned aside to a wonderful man, a very important bishop called Amator, who lived nearby. And there St. Patrick, knowing what was to happen to him, received the rank of bishop from the holy bishop Amator, as also Auxilius and Iserninus and others received lesser orders on the same day as St. Patrick was consecrated. They received the blessings, everything was performed in the customary way, and the following verse of the psalmist was also sung, especially appropriate for Patrick: 'You are a priest for ever, in the manner of Melchisedek.' (*Psalms 109.4*). Then in the name of the holy Trinity the venerable traveller went on board the ship which had been prepared and reached Britain; and as he made his way on foot he avoided all detours, except for the ordinary business of travelling (for no one seeks the Lord by idleness), and then he hurried across our sea with all speed and a favourable wind.

10. Now in the days in which these events took place in the aforesaid area there was a certain king, the fierce heathen emperor of the barbarians, who reigned in Tara, which was the Irish capital. His name was Loegaire, the son of Niall and the

ancestor of the royal house of almost the whole of this island. He had had wise men, wizards, soothsayers, enchanters and inventors of every black art who were able in their heathen, idolatrous way to know and foresee everything before it happened; two of them were favoured above the rest, their names being Lothroch, also called Lochru, and Lucetmael, also known as Ronal.

These two repeatedly foretold by their magical arts that there would come to be a certain foreign practice like a kingdom, with some strange and troublesome doctrine; a practice brought from afar across the seas, proclaimed by a few, adopted by many and respected by all; it would overthrow kingdoms, kill kings who resisted, win over great crowds, destroy all their gods, and after driving out all the resources of their art it would reign for ever and ever. They also identified and foretold the man who would bring and urge this practice in the following words, often repeated by them in a sort of verse form, especially in the two or three years preceding Patrick's arrival. This is how the verse ran; the sense is less than clear because of the different character of the language:

'Adze-head shall come, with his crook-headed staff and his house with a hole in its head. He shall chant blasphemy from his table, from the eastern part of his house, and all his household will answer him: 'So be it, so be it!' (This can be expressed more clearly in our own language.) 'So when all these things happen, our kingdom, which is heathen, shall not stand.'

And this is just as it later turned out. For the worship of idols was wiped out on Patrick's arrival, and the catholic faith in Christ filled every corner of our land. So much for this topic; let us return to our subject. . . .

22. And St. Patrick, according to the Lord Jesus' command going and teaching all nations and baptizing them in the name

9

of the Father and of the Son and of the Holy Ghost, set out from Tara and preached, with the Lord working with him and confirming his words with the following signs.

3

Pangur Ban

Celtic Ireland was not all saints. Its poetry included epics far from saintly (and far too epic to include here) and short poems, of which this anonymous piece about a scholar and his white cat is a charming example.
Source: Robin Flower, *The Irish Tradition* (Oxford: Clarendon Press, 1947), 24-25. Reprinted by permission of Oxford University Press.

I and Pangur Ban my cat,
'Tis a like task we are at:
Hunting mice is his delight,
Hunting words I sit all night.

Better far than praise of men
'Tis to sit with book and pen;
Pangur bears me no ill will,
He too plies his simple skill.

'Tis a merry thing to see
At our tasks how glad are we,
When at home we sit and find
Entertainment to our mind.

Oftentimes a mouse will stray
In the hero Pangur's way;
Oftentimes my keen thought set
Take a meaning in its net.

'Gainst the wall he sets his eye
Full and fierce and sharp and sly;
'Gainst the wall of knowledge I
All my little wisdom try.

When a mouse darts from its den
O how glad is Pangur then!
O what gladness do I prove
When I solve the doubts I love!

So in peace our tasks we ply,
Pangur Ban, my cat and I;
In our arts we find our bliss,
I have mine and he has his.

Practice every day has made
Pangur perfect in his trade;
I get wisdom day and night
Turning darkness into light.

4

The Bull *Laudabiliter,* 1155

Adrian IV (Nicholas Breakspear, 1154–1159) was the only English pope.
By this document he conferred on the English king the "lordship" of Ireland. The authenticity of the document has been questioned; the only text
is from a source close to Henry II. However, it is consistent with events,
and it was accepted by the Irish bishops at the Synod of Cashel, 1172.

Source: Edmund Curtis and R. B. McDowell, eds., *Irish Historical
Documents 1172–1922* (London: Routledge [Methuen & Co.], 1943), 17–
18; from Giraldus Cambrensis, *Expugnatio Hibernica*, Bk. II, ch. vi.

ADRIAN, bishop, servant of the servants of God, to our well-
beloved son in Christ the illustrious king of the English, greet-
ing and apostolic benediction.

Laudably and profitably does your majesty contemplate
spreading the glory of your name on earth and laying up for
yourself the reward of eternal happiness in heaven, in that, as
becomes a catholic prince, you purpose to enlarge the boundaries of the Church, to proclaim the truths of the Christian religion to a rude and ignorant people, and to root out the growths
of vice from the field of the Lord; and the better to accomplish
this purpose you seek the counsel and goodwill of the apostolic
see. In pursuing your object, the loftier your aim and the greater

your discretion, the more prosperous, we are assured, with God's assistance, will be the progress you will make: for undertakings commenced in the zeal of faith and the love of religion are ever wont to attain to a good end and issue. Verily, as your excellency doth acknowledge, there is no doubt that Ireland and all islands on which Christ the son of righteousness has shone, and which have accepted the doctrines of the Christian faith, belong to the jurisdiction of the blessed Peter and the holy Roman Church; wherefore the more pleased are we to plant in them the seed of faith acceptable to God, inasmuch as our conscience warns us that in their case a stricter account will hereafter be required of us.

Whereas then, well-beloved son in Christ, you have expressed to us your desire to enter the island of Ireland in order to subject its people to law and to root out from them the weeds of vice, and your willingness to pay an annual tribute to the blessed Peter of one penny from every house, and to maintain the rights of the churches of that land whole and inviolate: We therefore, meeting your pious and laudable desire with due favour and according a gracious assent to your petition, do hereby declare our will and pleasure that, with a view to enlarging the boundaries of the church, restraining the downward course of vice, correcting evil customs and planting virtue, and for the increase of the Christian religion, you shall enter that island and execute whatsoever may tend to the honour of God and the welfare of the land; and also that the people of that land shall receive you with honour and revere you as their lord: provided always that the rights of the churches remain whole and inviolate, and saving to the blessed Peter and the Holy Roman Church the annual tribute of one penny from every house. If then you should carry your project into effect, let it be your care to instruct that people in good ways of life, and so act, both in person and by agents whom you shall have found in faith, in word, and in deed fitted for the task, that the Church there may be adorned, that the Christian religion may take root and grow, and that all things appertaining to the honour of God and the salvation of souls may be so ordered that you may deserve at God's hands the fullness of an everlasting reward, and may obtain on earth a name renowned throughout the ages.

5

Treaty of Windsor, 1175

This treaty indicates what the English king and the Irish high king thought the "lordship" of Ireland meant. The boundary sketched here represents the outer limit of the first wave of English conquest; but it was soon disregarded by English adventurers and Irish chiefs alike.

Source: Curtis and McDowell, 22–24 (see document 4); from T. Rymer, *Foedera*, I:31, and other sources.

This is the agreement which was made at Windsor in the octaves of Michaelmas [October 6] in the year of Our Lord 1175, between Henry, king of England, and Roderick [Rory], king of Connaught, by Catholicus, archbishop of Tuam, Cantordis, abbot of Clonfert, and Master Laurence, chancellor of the king of Connaught, namely:

The king of England has granted to Roderic, his liegeman, king of Connacht, as long as he shall faithfully serve him, that he shall be king under him, ready to his service, as his man. And he shall hold his land as fully and as peacefully as he held it before the lord king entered Ireland, rendering him tribute. And that he shall have all the rest of the land and its inhabitants under him and shall bring them to account, so that they shall pay their full tribute to the king of England through him, and so that they shall maintain their rights. And those who are now in possession of their lands and rights shall hold them in peace as long as they remain in the fealty of the king of England, and continue to pay him faithfully and fully his tribute and the other rights which they owe to him, by the hand of the king of Connaught, saving in all things the right and honour of the king of England and of Roderic. And if any of them shall be rebels to the king of England and to Roderic and shall refuse to pay the tribute and other rights of the king of England by his hand, and shall withdraw from the fealty of the king of England, he, Roderic, shall judge them and remove them. And if he cannot answer for them by himself, the constable of the king of England in that land [Ireland] shall, when called upon by him, aid him to do what is necessary.

And for this agreement the said king of Connaught shall render to the king of England tribute every year, namely, out of every ten animals slaughtered, one hide, acceptable to the merchants both in his land as in the rest; save that he shall not meddle with those lands which the lord king has retained in his lordship and in the lordship of his barons; that is to say, Dublin with all its appurtenances; Meath with all its appurtenances, even as Murchat Ua Mailethlachlin [Murchadh O'Melaghlin] held it fully and freely or as others held it of him; Wexford with all its appurtenances, that is to say, the whole of Leinster; and Waterford with its whole territory from Waterford to Dungarvan, including Dungarvan with all its appurtenances.

And if the Irish who have fled wish to return to the land of the barons of the king of England they may do so in peace, paying the said tribute as others pay it, or doing to the English the services which they were wont to do for their lands, which shall be decided by the judgment and will of their lords. And if

17

any of them are unwilling to return and their lords have called upon the king of Connaught, he shall compel them to return to their land, so that they shall dwell there in peace.

And the king of Connaught shall accept hostages from all whom the lord king of England has committed to him, and he shall himself give hostages at the will of the king.

6

Statutes of Kilkenny, 1366

This enactment is infamous in Irish history for "outlawing" the native Irish, i.e., declaring them outside of English law. In fact, it represents a desperate effort by the English colonists ("the English born in Ireland") to preserve their national identity in the face of almost irresistible temptations to "go native" and of condescension by the mother country. They could think of no other way to do this than by imposing by law a system of apartheid and declaring noncomplying Irish (and English) outside the law.

Source: Curtis and McDowell, 52–59 (see document 4); from *Statutes and ordinances and acts of the parliament of Ireland, King John to Henry V*, ed. H. F. Berry, 431–69 (French).

Whereas at the conquest of the land of Ireland and for a long time after, the English of the said land used the English language, mode of riding and apparel and were governed and ruled, they and their subjects called *Betaghes*, by the English law. . . . But now many English of the said land, forsaking the English language, fashion, mode of riding, laws, and usages, live and govern themselves according to the manners, fashion and language of the Irish enemies, and also have made divers marriages and alliances between themselves and the Irish enemies aforesaid; whereby the said land and the liege people thereof, the

English language, the allegiance due to our lord the King, and the English laws there are put in subjection and decayed and the Irish enemies exalted and raised up contrary to right. Now therefore our lord the King, considering the mischiefs aforesaid, in consequence of the grievous complaints of the commons of his said land summoned to his Parliament held at Kilkenny the Thursday next after Ash Wednesday in the fortieth year of his reign, before his well-beloved son Lionel, Duke of Clarence, his Lieutenant in Ireland, to the honour of God and of his glorious Mother and of Holy Church and for the good government of the said land and quiet of the people and for the better observance of the laws and the punishment of evil doers, there are ordained and established by our said lord the King and his said Lieutenant and council there with the assent of the archbishops, bishops, abbots and priors . . . the Earls, barons, and others the commons of the said land at the said parliament there assembled the ordinances and articles under-written to be held and kept perpetually, upon the penalties contained therein.

. . . it is ordained and established that no alliance by marriage, gossipred, fostering of children, concubinage or amour or in any other manner be henceforth made between the English and Irish on the one side or on the other. And that no Englishman or other person being at peace shall give or sell to any Irish in time of peace or war horses or armour or any manner of victuals in time of war. And if any do to the contrary and thereof be attaint, that he shall have judgment of life and limb as a traitor to our lord the King.

Also it is ordained and established that every Englishman shall use the English language and be named by an English name, leaving off entirely the manner of naming used by the Irish; and that every Englishman use the English custom, fashion, mode of riding and apparel according to his estate; and if any English or Irish living amongst the English use the Irish language amongst themselves contrary to this ordinance and thereof be attaint, that his lands and tenements, if he have any, be seized into the hands of his immediate lord until he come to one of the places of our lord the King and find sufficient surety to adopt and use the English language and then that he have restitution of his said lands by writ to issue out of the same place. . . . And that no Englishman who has to the value of one hundred shillings of lands or tenements or of rent by the year shall ride otherwise than on a saddle in the English fashion, and he that shall do the contrary and be thereof attaint his horse shall be forfeited to our lord the King and his body committed to prison until he make fine according to the King's pleasure for the contempt aforesaid. And also that beneficed persons of Holy Church living amongst the English shall use the English language; and if they do not, then their ordinaries shall have the issues of their benefices until they use the English language as aforesaid; and they shall have respite in order to learn the English language and to provide saddles between this and the feast of Saint Michael next coming.

Also, whereas diversity of government and divers laws in one land cause diversity of allegiance and disputes among the people, it is agreed and established that no English having disputes with other English henceforth make distraint or take pledge, distress, or vengeance against any other whereby the people may be troubled, but that they shall sue each other at the common law, and that no English be governed in the settlement of their disputes by March or Brehon law, which by right ought not be called law but bad custom; but that they be governed by the common law of the land as the lieges of our lord the King; and if any do to the contrary and thereof be attaint then he shall be taken and imprisoned and adjudged as a traitor. And that no difference of allegiance henceforth be made between the English born in Ireland and the English born in England by calling them 'English hobbe' or 'Irish dog,' but that all shall be called by one name [viz.] the English lieges of our lord the King. . . .

Also, whereas a land which is at war requires that every person do render himself able to defend himself, it is ordained and established that the commons of the said land of Ireland who are in divers marches of war use not henceforth the games which men call 'hurlings' with great clubs at ball upon the ground, from which great evils and maims have arisen to the weakening of the defence of the said land, and other games which men call 'coitings,' but that they apply and accustom themselves to use and draw bows and throw lances and other gentle games which appertain to arms, whereby the Irish enemies may be the better checked by the liege commons of these parts. . . .

Also it is ordained that no Irish of the nations of the Irish shall be admitted into any cathedral or collegiate church by provision, collation, or presentation of any person whatsoever or to any benefice of Holy Church amongst the English of the land. . . .

Also it is agreed and established that no house of religion which is situate among the English, whether it be exempt or not, shall henceforth receive any Irishmen [to their] profession but shall receive Englishmen, without taking into consideration that they be born in England or in Ireland. . . .

Also, whereas the Irish minstrels coming among the English spy out the secrets, customs and policies of the English whereby great evils have often happened, it is agreed and forbidden that any Irish minstrels, that is to say tympanours, poets, story-tellers, babblers, rymours, harpers or any other Irish minstrels shall come amongst the English; and that no English receive them or make gift to them. . . .

7

Poynings' Law (1494)

This law, passed by the Irish parliament at the instance of an English governor, effectively ended the independence of the Irish parliament and subordinated it to the English government until its repeal in 1782.
Source: *Statutes at Large, Ireland*, I: 44; 10 Henry VII, c. 4.

An Act that no Parliament be holden in this Land until the Acts be certified into England.

Item, at the request of the commons of the land of Ireland, be it ordained, enacted and established that . . . no Parliament be holden hereafter in the said land, but at such season as the King's lieutenant and counsaile there first do certifie the King, under the great seal of that land, the causes and considerations, and all such acts as them seemeth should pass in the same Parliament, and such causes, considerations, and acts, affirmed by the King and his counsail to be good and expedient for that land, and his licence thereupon, as well in affirmation of the said causes and acts, as to summon the said Parliament under his great seal of England had and obtained; that done, a Parliament to be had and holden after the form and effect afore rehearsed: and if any Parliament be holden in that land hereafter, contrary to the form and provision aforesaid, it be deemed void and of none effect in law.

8

Act of Uniformity, 1560

This is the definitive act by which the Anglican Church was set up as the official Church of Ireland. Though enacted by the Irish Parliament, it adopts the Book of Common Prayer of the Church of England, written in English.

Source: *Statutes at Large, Ireland*, I: 284–90; 2 Eliz. I, c. 2.

An Act for the Uniformitie of Common Prayer and Service in the Church, and the Administration of the Sacraments

Where at the death of our late soverain lord King Edward the 6. there remained one uniforme order of common service, prayer and the administration of sacraments, rites and ceremonies in the church of England, which was set forth in one book, intituled, "The Book of Common Prayer, and administration of Sacraments" which was repealed and taken away by act of Parliament in the said realm of England in the first year of the raign of our late soveraign lady Queen Mary, to the great decay of the true honour of God, and discomfort to the professors of the truth of Christ's religion. Be it therefore enacted by the authoritie of this present Parliament. That the said book with the order of service, and of the administration of sacraments, rites and ceremonies, with the alterations and additions therein added and appointed by this estatute, shall stand and bee from and after the feast of Pentecost, next ensuing, in full force and effect, . . .

II. And further be it enacted . . . that all and singular ministers in any cathedrall or parish church, or other place within this realm of Ireland, shall from and after the feast of Saint John Baptist, then next ensuing, be bounden to say and use the mattens, evensong, celebration of the Lord's supper, and administration of each of the sacraments, and all their common and open prayer, in such order and form as is mentioned in the said book. . . .

9

Edmund Spenser: A View of the State of Ireland (1595)

The great poet Edmund Spenser served in the English government of Ireland and obtained an estate there. He wrote this pamphlet shortly after the beginning of Tyrone's rebellion. It is in the form of a dialogue between Eudoxus and Ireneus (Spenser himself). It has some interest as a description of Ireland for Englishmen, but it is marred by Spenser's etymological fancies and his English prejudices, particularly the assumption that everybody ought to be like the English. His proposal for a large plantation and resettlement anticipates the plantation of Ulster, though it is more far-reaching. The spelling of this edition has been modernized, but the style is original.

Source: The Works of Edmund Spenser (London: Henry Washbourne, 1845), 478–530.

Eudox.–But if that country of Ireland, whence you lately came, be of so goodly and commodious a soil, as you report, I wonder that no course is taken for the turning thereof to good uses, and reducing that nation to better government and civility.

Iren.–Marry, so there have been divers good plots devised, and wise counsels cast already about reformation of that realm; but they say, it is the fatal destiny of that land, that no purposes whatsoever which are meant for her good, will prosper or take good effect. . . .

Iren.–I will then, according to your advisement, begin to declare the evils which seem to me most hurtful to the commonweal of that land; and first, those (I say) which were most ancient and long grown; and they also are of three sorts: the first in the laws, the second in customs, and the last in religion.

. . . it is a nation ever acquainted with wars, though but amongst themselves, and in their own kind of military discipline, trained up ever from their youths; which they have never yet been taught to lay aside, nor made to learn obedience unto laws, scarcely to know the name of law, but instead thereof have always preserved and kept their own law, which is the Brehon law.

Eudox.–What is that which you call the Brehon law? It is a word unto us altogether unknown.

Iren.–It is a rule of right unwritten, but delivered by tradition from one to another, in which oftentimes there appeareth great shew of equity, in determining the right between party and party, but in many things repugning quite both to God's law and man's: as for example, in the case of murder, the Brehon, that is their judge, will compound between the murderer and the friends of the party murdered, which prosecute the action, that the malefactor shall give unto them, or to the child or wife of him that is slain, a recompense, which they call an Eriach; by which vile law of theirs, many murders amongst them are made up and smothered.

. . . there be many wide countries in Ireland which the laws of England were never established in, nor any acknowledgment of subjection made; and also even in those which are subdued, and seem to acknowledge subjection, yet the same Brehon law is practised among themselves, by reason, that dwelling as they do, whole nations and septs of the Irish together, without any Englishman among them, they may do what they list. . . .

Eudox.–What is this which you call *Tanist* and *Tanistry*? They be names and terms never heard of nor known to us.

Iren.–It is a custom amongst all the Irish, that presently after the death of any of their chief lords or captains, they do presently assemble themselves to a place generally appointed and known unto them, to choose another in his stead, where they do nominate and elect, for the most part, not the eldest son, nor any of the children of the lord deceased, but the next to him of blood, that is, the eldest and worthiest; as commonly the next brother unto him, if he have any, or the next cousin, or so forth, as any is elder in that kindred or sept: and then next to him do they choose the next of the blood to be *Tanist*, who shall next succeed him in the said captainry, if he live thereunto.

. . . when the Earl Strongbow having conquered that land, delivered up the same into the hands of Henry the Second, then King; who sent over thither a great store of gentlemen, and other warlike people, amongst whom he distributed the land, and settled such a strong colony therein, as never since could, with all the subtle practices of the Irish, be rooted out; but abide still a mighty people, of so many as remain English of them.

Eudox.–What is this that you say, of so many as remain English of them? Why, are not they that were once English, English still?

Iren.–No, for some of them are degenerated, and grown mere Irish; yea, and more malicious to the English, than the Irish themselves.

Eudox.–What heard I? And is it possible that an Englishman, brought up in such sweet civility as England affords, should find such liking in that barbarous rudeness, that he should forget his own nature, and forego his own nation? . . .

Iren.–I suppose that the chief cause of bringing in the Irish language amongst them, was specially their fostering and marrying with the Irish, the which are two most dangerous infections: for first, the child that sucketh the milk of the nurse, must of necessity learn his first speech of her: the which being the first inured to his tongue, is ever after most pleasing unto him: insomuch, as though he afterwards be taught English, yet the smack of the first will always abide with him; and not only of the speech, but also of the manners and conditions. . . . Therefore are these evil customs of fostering and marrying with the Irish, most carefully to be restrained: for of them two, the third evil, that is, the custom of language (which I spoke of), chiefly proceedeth. . . .

Iren.–There is amongst the Irish a certain kind of people called bards, which are to them instead of poets, whose profession is to set forth the praises or dispraises of men in their poems or rhythms, the which are had in so high regard and estimation amongst them, that none dare displease them, for fear to run into reproach through their offence, and to be made infamous in the mouths of all men. For their verses are taken up with a general applause, and usually sung at all feasts and meetings by certain other persons, whose proper function that is, who also receive for the same great rewards and reputation amongst them. . . .

But these Irish bards are for the most part of another mind, and so far from instructing young men in moral discipline, that they themselves do more deserve to be sharply disciplined: for they seldom use to choose unto themselves the doings of good men for the arguments of their poems, but whomsoever they find to be most licentious of life, most bold and lawless in his doings, most dangerous and desperate in all parts of disobedience and rebellious disposition; him they set up and glorify in their rhymes; him they praise to the people, and to young men make an example to follow.

Now we will proceed to other like defects, amongst which there is one general inconvenience, which reigneth almost throughout all Ireland; that is, the lords of land and freeholders do not there use to set out their land in farm, or for term of years, to their tenants, but only from year to year, and some during pleasure; neither indeed will the Irish tenant or husbandman otherwise take his land, than so long as he list himself. . . .

Iren.—Marry, the evils which come hereby are great; for by this means both the landlord thinketh that he hath his tenant more at command, to follow him into what action soever he shall enter, and also the tenant being left at his liberty, is fit for every occasion of change that shall be offered by time; and so much also the more ready and willing is he to run into the same; for that he hath no such state in any his holding, no such building upon any farm, no such cost employed in fencing or husbanding the same, as might withhold him from any such wilful course as his lord's cause, or his own lewd disposition may carry him unto. All which he hath forborne, and spared so much expense; for that he had no firm estate in his tenement, but was only a tenant at will, or little more, and so at will may leave it.

. . . the fault which I find in religion is but one; but the same is universal throughout all that country; that is, that they be all papists by their profession, but in the same so blindly and brutishly informed (for the most part) that not one amongst a hundred knoweth any ground of religion, or any article of his faith; but can perhaps say his Paternoster, or his Ave-Maria, without any knowledge or understanding what one word thereof meaneth.

. . . yet what good should any English minister do amongst them, by teaching or preaching to them, which either cannot understand him, or will not hear him? or what comfort of life shall he have, where his parishioners are so insatiable, so intractable, so ill-affected to him, as they usually be to all the English?

30

. . . all change is to be shunned, where the affairs stand in such sort, as that they may continue in quietness, or be assured at all to abide as they are, but that in the realm of Ireland we see much otherwise; for every day we perceive the troubles growing more upon us, and one evil growing upon another; insomuch, as there is no part now found or ascertained, but all have their ears upright, waiting when the watch-word shall come, that they should all arise generally into rebellion, and cast away the English subjection. To which there now little wanteth; for I think the word be already given, and there wanteth nothing but opportunity. . . all the realm is first to be reformed, and laws are afterwards to be made, for keeping and continuing it in that reformed estate.

Eudox.—How then do you think is there formation thereof to be begun, if not by laws and ordinances?

Iren.—Even by the sword; for all these evils must first be cut away by a strong hand, before any good can be planted.

. . . by the sword, I mean, the royal power of the prince, which ought to stretch itself forth in the chiefest strength, to the redressing and cutting off those evils which I before blamed. . . .

The first thing must be, to send over into that realm such a strong power of men, as should perforce bring in all that rebellious rout and loose people, which either do now stand out in open arms, or wandering in companies, do keep the woods, spoiling the good subjects.

Eudox.—You speak now, Ireneus, of an infinite charge to her Majesty, to send over such an army as should tread down all that standeth before them on foot, and lay on the ground all the stiff-necked people of that land: for there is now but one outlaw of any great reckoning, to wit, the Earl of Tyrone, abroad in arms; against whom, you see, what huge charges she hath been at this last year, in sending of men, providing of victuals, and making head against him; yet there is little or nothing at all

31

done, but the queen's treasure spent, her people wasted, the poor country troubled, and the enemy nevertheless brought into no more subjection than he was, or list outwardly to show, which in effect is none, but rather a scorn of her power, and emboldening of a proud rebel, and an encouragement to all like lewdly-disposed traitors, that shall dare to lift up their heel against their sovereign lady.

. . . all the lands will I give unto Englishmen, whom I will have drawn thither, who shall have the same, with such estates as shall be thought meet, and for such rent as shall eftsoons be rated. Under every of those Englishmen will I place some of those Irish to be tenants, for a certain rent, according to the quantity of such land as every man shall have allotted unto him, and shall be found able to wield; wherein this special regard shall be had, that in no place under any landlord, there shall be many of them placed together, but dispersed wide from their acquaintance, and scattered far abroad through all the country. For that is the evil which now I find in all Ireland, that the Irish dwell altogether by their septs, and several nations, so as they may practise or conspire what they will: whereas if there were English well placed among them, they should not be able once to stir or to murmur, but that it should be known, and they shortened according to their demerits.

10

Tyrone's Demands (1599)

Hugh O'Neill, Earl of Tyrone, in his great but ultimately unsuccessful revolt, set forth his goals in a document which sums up the grievances of Irish Catholics. This copy was endorsed by the English minister Sir Robert Cecil with the word "Ewtopia."

Source: Curtis and McDowell, 119–20 (see document 4); from Calendar of State Papers relating to Ireland, 1599–1600 (London, 1899), 279–81.

Articles Intended to be Stood Upon by Tyrone

1. That the Catholic, Apostolic, and Roman religion be openly preached and taught throughout all Ireland, as well in cities as borough towns, by Bishops, seminary priests, Jesuits, and all other religious men.

2. That the Church of Ireland be wholly governed by the Pope.

3. That all cathedrals and parish churches, abbeys, and all other religious houses, with all tithes and church lands, now in the hands of the English, be presently restored to the Catholic churchmen.

4. That all Irish priests and religious men, now prisoners in England or Ireland, be presently set at liberty, with all temporal Irishmen, that are troubled for their conscience, and to go where they will without further trouble.

5. That all Irish priests and religious men may freely pass and repass, by sea and land, to and from foreign countries.

6. That no Englishman may be a churchman in Ireland.

7. That there be erected an university upon the Crown rents of Ireland, wherein all sciences shall be taught according to the manner of the Catholic Roman Church.

8. That the Governor of Ireland be at least an Earl, and of the Privy Council of England, bearing the name of Viceroy.

9. That the Lord Chancellor, Lord Treasurer, Lord Admiral, the Council of State, the Justices of the laws, Queen's Attorney, Queen's Serjeant, and all other officers appertaining to the Council and law of Ireland, be Irishmen.

10. That all principal governments of Ireland, as Connaught, Munster, etc., be governed by Irish noblemen.

11. That the Master of Ordnance, and half the soldiers with their officers resident in Ireland, be Irishmen.

12. That no Irishman's heirs shall lose their lands for the faults of their ancestors.

13. That no Irishman's heir under age shall fall in the Queen's or her successors' hands, as a ward, but that the living be put to the heir's profit, and the advancement of his younger brethren, and marriages of his sisters, if he have any.

14. That no children nor any other friends be taken as pledges for the good abearing of their parents, and, if there be any such pledges now in the hands of the English, they must presently be released.

15. That all statutes made against the preferment of Irishmen as well in their own country as abroad, be presently recalled.

16. That the Queen nor her successors may in no sort press an Irishman to serve them against his will.

17. That O'Neill, O'Donnell, the Earl of Desmond, with all their partakers, may peaceable enjoy all lands and privi-

leges that did appertain to their predecessors 200 years past.

18. That all Irishmen, of what quality they be, may freely travel in foreign countries, for their better experience, without making any of the Queen's officers acquainted withal.

19. That all Irishmen may freely travel and traffic all merchandises in England as Englishmen, paying the same rights and tributes as the English do.

20. That all Irishmen may freely traffic with all merchandises, that shall be thought necessary by the Council of State of Ireland for the profit of their Republic, with foreigners or in foreign countries, and no Irishman shall be troubled for the passage of priests or other religious men.

21. That all Irishmen that will may learn, and use all occupations and arts whatsoever.

22. That all Irishmen may freely build ships of what burden they will, furnishing the same with artillery and all munition at their pleasure.

11

Plantation of Ulster, 1610

These conditions represent a deliberate plan not only to change land ownership but to settle English and Scottish Protestant colonists under frontier
conditions. This selection relates to the major English and Scottish planters ("undertakers" because they undertook these commitments). Other provisions dealt with lesser planters ("servitors") and selected "natives," who
were under fewer obligations as to colonizing.

Source: Curtis and McDowell, 128–31 (see document 4); from *Bulletin
of the Institute of Historical Research*, 12 (February 1935), 178–83.

Conditions to be observed by the British undertakers of the escheated lands in Ulster, etc.

1. What the British undertakers shall have.

First, the lands to be undertaken by them, are divided into sun-
dry precincts of different quantities.

Every precinct is subdivided into proportions of three sorts,
great, middle, and small.

The great proportion containeth 2000 English acres at the least.

The middle proportion containeth 1500 acres at the least.

The small proportion containeth 1000 acres at the least.

Unto every of which proportions such bog and wood shall be allowed, as lieth within the same, for which no rent shall be reserved.

The precincts are by name distinguished, part for the English, and part for the Scottish, as appeareth by the table of distribution of the precincts.

Every precinct shall be assigned to one principal undertaker and his consort, as will appear by the table of assignation of the precincts.

The chief undertakers shall be allowed two middle proportions if they desire the same; otherwise no one undertaker is to be allowed above one great proportion.

They shall have an estate in fee simple to them and their heirs.

They shall have power to create manors, to hold courts baron twice every year and not oftener, and power to create tenures in socage to hold of themselves. . . .

2. *What the said undertakers shall for their parts perform.*

They shall yearly yield unto his majesty for every proportion of 1000 acres, five pound six shillings eight pence English, and so rateably for the great proportions; the first half year's payment to begin at Michaelmas 1614.

Every of the said undertakers shall hold the lands so undertaken in free and common socage, as of the castle of Dublin, and by no greater service.

Every of the said undertakers of a great proportion, shall within 3 years to be accounted from Easter next, build thereupon a stone house, with a strong court or bawn about it; and every undertaker of a middle proportion shall within the same time build a stone or brick house thereupon, with a strong court or bawn about it; and every undertaker of a small proportion, shall within the same time make thereupon a strong court or bawn at least.

Every undertaker shall within three years, to be accounted from Easter next, plant or place upon a small proportion, the number of 24 able men of the age of 18 years or upwards, being English or inland Scottish; and so rateably upon the other proportions; which numbers shall be reduced into 10 families at least, to be settled upon every small proportion, and rateably upon the other proportions, in this manner, viz. the principal undertaker and his family to be settled upon a demesne of 300 acres, two fee-farmers upon 120 acres a piece, three leaseholders for three lives or 21 years upon 100 acres a piece, and upon the residue being 160 acres, four families or more of husbandmen, artificers or cottagers, their portions of land to be assigned by the principal undertaker at his discretion.

Every of the said undertakers shall draw their tenants to build houses for themselves and their families, not scattering, but together, near the principal house or bawn, as well for their mutual defence and strength, as for the making of villages and townships.

The said undertakers, their heirs and assigns, shall have ready in the houses at all times, a convenient store of arms, wherewith they may furnish a competent number of men for their defence, which may be viewed and mustered every half year according to the manner of England.

Every of the said undertakers before he be received to be an undertaker, shall take the oath of supremacy . . . and shall also conform themselves in religion according to his majesty's laws; and every of their undertenants being chief of a family, shall take the like oath. . . . And they and their families shall also be conformable in religion, as aforesaid. . . .

The said undertakers, their heirs and assigns, shall not alien or demise their portions or any part thereof to the mere Irish, or to such persons as will not take the said oath of supremacy. . . .

12

Confederation of Kilkenny, 1642

Voted by an assembly of Catholic lords, bishops, gentry and clergy, meeting at Kilkenny (since Dublin was in Protestant hands), this amounts to a constitution for a Catholic state of Ireland. The lawyers who drafted it show a concern for legality while institutionalizing a rebellion.

Source: Curtis and McDowell, 148–52 (see document 4); from Gilbert MSS, 219 (Pearse St. Public Library).

Orders made and established by the lords spiritual and temporal, and the rest of the general assembly for the kingdom of Ireland, met at the city of Kilkenny, the 24th day of October, Anno Domini 1642, and in the eighteenth year of the reign of our sovereign lord, King Charles, by the grace of God, of Great Britain, France and Ireland, etc.

I. Imprimis that the Roman catholic church in Ireland shall and may have and enjoy the privileges and immunities according to the great charter, made and declared within the realm of England, in the ninth year of King Henry III, sometime king of England, and the lord of Ireland, and afterwards enacted and confirmed in this realm of Ireland. And that the common law of

England, and all the statutes of force in this kingdom, which are not against the Roman catholic religion, or the liberties of the natives, and other liberties of this kingdom, shall be observed throughout the whole kingdom, and that all proceedings in civil and criminal cases shall be according to the same laws.

II. Item, that all and every person and persons within this kingdom shall bear faith and true allegiance unto our sovereign lord King Charles . . . his heirs and lawful successors, and shall uphold and maintain his and their rights and lawful prerogatives, . . .

III. Item, that the common laws of England and Ireland, and the said statutes, called the great charter, and every clause, branch and article thereof, and all other statutes confirming, expounding or declaring the same, shall be punctually observed within this kingdom, so far forth as the condition of the present times, during these times, can by possibilities give way thereunto, and after the war is ended the same to be observed without any limitations, or restriction whatsoever.

IV. . . . For the exaltation therefore of the holy Roman catholic church, for the advancement of his majesty's service, and the preservation of the lives, estates, and liberties of his majesty's true subjects of this kingdom against the injustice, murders, massacres, rapes, depredations, robberies, burnings, frequent breaches of public faith and quarters, and destruction daily perpetrated and acted upon his majesty's said subjects, and advised, contrived, and daily executed by the malignant party, some of them managing the government and affairs of state in Dublin, and some other parts of this kingdom, to his majesty's greatest disservice, and complying with their confederates, the malignant party in England and elsewhere, who (as it is manifest to all the world) do complot, and practise to dishonour and destroy his majesty, his royal consort the queen, their issue, and the monarchial government, which is of most dangerous consequence to all the monarchs and princes of Christendom, the said assembly doth order and establish a council by name of a supreme council of the confederate catholics of Ireland, who are to consist of the number of four and twenty to be forthwith named, whereof twelve at the least, to be forthwith named, shall reside in this kingdom, or where else they shall think expedient, and the members of the said council shall have equal votes, and two parts of three or more concurring present votes, to conclude, and not fewer to sit in council than nine, whereof seven at least are to concur; and of the four and twenty a president shall be named by the assembly, to be one of the said twelve resident. . . . And the said council shall have the power and pre-eminence following, viz. the lords general and all other commanders of armies, and civil magistrates and officers in the several provinces shall observe their orders and decrees, and shall do nothing contrary to their directions, and shall give them speedy advertisement and account of their proceedings. . . .

That the said council shall have power and authority to do and execute all manner of acts and things conducing to the advancement of the catholic cause, and good of this kingdom, and concerning the war, as if done by the assembly, and shall have power to hear and determine all matters capital, criminal or civil, excepting the right or title of land. . . .

V. Item, it is further ordered and established, that in every province of this kingdom there shall be a provincial council, and in every county a county council. . . .

XII. Item, it is further ordered, that whosoever hath entered since the first day of October, 1641, or shall hereafter during the continuance of the war in this kingdom, enter into the lands, tenements, or hereditaments, at or immediately before the first day of October. . . shall immediately restore upon demand, the said possession to the party or parties so put out. . . provided, and so it is meant, that if any of the parties so put out, be declared a neuter or enemy by the supreme or provincial council, then the party who gained the possession as aforesaid shall give up the possession to such person or persons, as shall be named either by the said council provincial, or supreme council, to be disposed of towards the maintenance of the general cause, . . .

XIV. Item, for the avoiding of national distinction between the subjects of his Majesty's dominions, which this assembly doth utterly detest and abhor, and which ought not to be endured in a well-governed commonwealth, it is ordered and established, that, upon pain of the highest punishment, which may be inflicted by authority of this assembly, that every Roman catholic, as well English, Welsh, as Scotch, who was of that profession before the troubles, and who will come and please to reside in this kingdom and join in the present union, shall be preserved and cherished in his life, goods, and estates, by the power, authority, and force (if need require it) of all the catholics of Ireland, as fully and as freely as any native born therein, and shall be acquitted and eased of one third part (in three parts to be divided) of public charges or levies raised or to be raised for the maintenance of this holy war.

XV. Item, and it is further ordered and established, that there shall be no distinction or comparison made betwixt Old Irish, and Old and New English or betwixt septs or families, or betwixt citizens and townsmen and countrymen, joining in union, upon pain of the highest punishment that can be inflicted by any of the councils aforesaid, according to the nature and quality of the offences, and division like to spring thence. . . .

XXVI. Item, it is ordered and established, that the possession of protestant archbishops, bishops, deans, dignitaries, and parsons, in right of their respective churches, or their tenements in the beginning of these troubles, shall be deemed, taken, and construed as the possession of the catholic archbishops, bishops, deans, dignitaries, pastors and their tenements respectively. . . .

13

Oliver Cromwell:
The Capture of Drogheda
(1649)

This is Cromwell's report to the Speaker of the House of Commons, the highest authority then in England. The massacre is described with a sincere self-righteousness. The event was appalling, but the effect was decisive.
Source: Thomas Carlyle, *The Letters and Speeches of Oliver Cromwell*, ed. S.C. Lomas, 3 vols. (London, 1904), I: 466–71; dated September 17, 1649.

For the Honourable William Lenthall, Esquire, Speaker of the Parliament of England: These

SIR,

Your Army came before the town upon Monday following, where having pitched, as speedy course was taken as could be to frame our batteries, which took up the more time because divers of the battering guns were on shipboard. Upon Monday the 9th of this instant, the batteries began to play. Whereupon I sent Sir Arthur Ashton, the then Governor, a summons to deliver the town to the use of the Parliament of England. To the which I received no satisfactory answer, but proceeded that day to beat down the steeple of the church on the south side of town, and to beat down a tower not far from the same place. . . .

The enemy retreated, diverse of them, into the Mill-Mount; a place very strong and of difficult access, being exceedingly high, having a good graft, and strongly palisadoed. The Governor, Sir Arthur Ashton, and diverse considerable Officers being there, our men getting up to them, were ordered by me to put them all to the sword. And indeed, being in the heat of action, I forbade them to spare any that were in arms in the town, and, I think, that night they put to the sword about 2,000 men, divers of the officers and soldiers being fled over the Bridge into the other part of the Town, were about one hundred of them possessed St. Peter's church-steeple, some the west gate, and others a strong round tower next the gate called St. Sunday's. These being summoned to yield to mercy, refused, whereupon I ordered the steeple of St. Peter's Church to be fired, where one of them was heard to say in the midst of the flames: "God damn me, God confound me; I burn, I burn."

The next day, the other two towers were summoned, in one of which was about six or seven score; but they refused to yield themselves, and we knowing that hunger must compel them, set only good guard to secure them from running away until their stomach were come down. From one of the said towers, notwithstanding their condition, they killed and wounded some of our men. When they submitted, their officers were knocked on the head, and every tenth man of the soldiers killed, and the rest shipped for the Barbadoes. The soldiers in the other tower were all spared, as to their lives only, and shipped likewise for the Barbadoes.

I am persuaded that this is a righteous judgment of God upon these barbarous wretches, who have imbrued their hands in so much innocent blood; and that it will tend to prevent the effusion of blood for the future, which are the satisfactory grounds to such actions, which otherwise cannot but work remorse and regret. . . .

And now give me leave to say how it comes to pass that this work is wrought. It was set upon some of our hearts, That a great thing should be done, not by power or might, but by the Spirit of God. And is it not so clear? That which caused your men to storm so courageously, it was the Spirit of God, who gave your men courage, and took it away again; and gave the enemy courage, and took it away again; and gave your men courage again, and therewith this happy success. And therefore it is good that God alone have all the glory.

It is remarkable that these people, at the first, set up the mass in some places of the town that had been monasteries; but afterwards grew so insolent that, the last Lord's day before the storm, the Protestants were thrust out of the great Church called St. Peter's, and they had public mass there: and in this very place near one thousand of them were put to the sword, fleeing thither for safety. I believe all their friars were knocked on the head promiscuously but two; the one of which was Father Peter Taaff, (brother to the Lord Taaff), whom the soldiers took, the next day, and made an end of; the other was taken in the round tower, under the repute of lieutenant, and when he understood that the officers in that tower had no quarter, he confessed that he was a friar; but that did not save him. . . .

14

Treaty of Limerick, Civil Articles, 1691

The Treaty of Limerick (strictly speaking, a capitulation, not a treaty) completed the Williamite reconquest of Ireland. The military articles were fulfilled; but the refusal of the Irish Parliament to ratify most of the civil articles opened the gates for the passage of penal laws against Roman Catholics. Only article 2 was ratified; the others were not, nor was the key passage in the king's letters patent which follow.

Source: Curtis and McDowell, 171–75 (see document 4); from *The civil articles of Limerick exactly printed from the letters patent* (Dublin, 1692).

In consideration of the surrender of the city of Limerick and other agreements made between the said Lieutenant-General Ginckle, the governor of the city of Limerick, and the generals of the Irish army, bearing date with these presents, for the surrender of the said city, and submission of the said army, it is agreed, that:

1. The Roman catholics of this kingdom, shall enjoy such privileges in the exercise of their religion, as are consistent with the laws of Ireland, or as they did enjoy in the reign of King Charles II, and their majesties, as soon as their affairs will permit them to summon a parliament in this kingdom, will endeav-

our to procure the said Roman catholics such farther security in that particular, as may preserve them from any disturbance upon the account of their said religion.

2. All the inhabitants or residents of Limerick, or any other garrison now in the possession of the Irish, and all officers and soldiers, now in arms, under any commission of King James, or those authorized by him to grant the same in the several counties of Limerick, Clare, Kerry, Cork, and Mayo, or any of them, and all the commissioned officers in their majesties' quarters, that belong to the Irish regiments, now in being, that are treated with, and who are not prisoners of war or have taken protection, and who shall return and submit to their majesties' obedience, and their and every of their heirs, shall hold, possess and enjoy all and every their estates of free-hold, and inheritance, and all the rights, titles, and interests, privileges and immunities, which they, and every, or any of them held, enjoyed, or were rightfully and lawfully entitled to in the reign of King Charles II, or at any time since, by the laws and statutes that were in force in the said reign of King Charles II, and shall be put in possession, by order of the government, of such of them as are in the king's hands or the hands of his tenants, without being put to any suit or trouble therein; and all such estates shall be freed and discharged from all arrears of crown-rents, quit-rents, and other public charges incurred and become due since Michaelmas 1688, to the day of the date hereof. And all persons comprehended in this article, shall have, hold, and enjoy all their goods and chattels, real and personal, to them, or any of them belonging, and remaining either in their own hands, or the hands of any persons whatsoever, in trust for or for the use of them, or any of them; ... provided, that nothing in this article contained, be construed to extend to or restore any forfeiting person now out of the kingdom, except what are hereafter comprised. Provided also, that

no person whatsoever shall have or enjoy the benefit of this article, that shall neglect or refuse to take the oath of allegiance made by act of parliament in England, in the first year of the reign of their present majesties, when thereunto required. . . .

7. Every nobleman and gentleman, comprised in the said second and third article, shall have liberty to ride with a sword, and case of pistols, if they think fit, and keep a gun in their houses, for the defence of the same or for fowling. . . .

12. Lastly, the lords justices and general do undertake, that their majesties will ratify these articles within the space of eight months, or sooner, and use their utmost endeavours, that the same shall be ratified and confirmed in parliament. . . .

For the true performance hereof, we have hereunto set our hands,

Char. Porter, Tho. Coningsby, Bar. De Ginckle.

And whereas the said city of Limerick hath been since, in pursuance of the said articles, surrendered unto us. Now know ye, that we having considered of the said articles are graciously pleased hereby to declare, that we do for us, our heirs and successors, as far as in us lies, ratify and confirm the same, and every clause, matter and thing therein contained. And as to such parts thereof, for which an act of parliament shall be found to be necessary, we shall recommend the same to be made good by parliament, and shall give our royal assent to any bill or bills that shall be passed by our two houses of parliament to that purpose. And whereas it appears unto us, that it was agreed between the parties to the said articles, that after the words, 'Limerick, Clare, Kerry, Cork, Mayo,' or any of them in the second of such articles, the words following; viz. 'And all such as are under their protection in the said counties,' should be inserted, and be part of the said articles. Which words having been casually omitted by the writer, the omission was not discovered till after the said articles were signed, but was taken notice before the second town was surrendered; and that our said justices, and general or one of them, did promise that the said clause should be made good, it being within the intention of the capitulation, and inserted in the foul draught thereof. Our further will and pleasure is, and we do hereby ratify and confirm the said omitted words, viz. 'And all such as are under their protection in the said counties' hereby for us, our heirs and successors, ordaining and declaring, that all and every person and persons therein concerned, shall and may have, receive, and enjoy the benefit thereof, in such and the same manner, as if the said words had been inserted in their proper place, in the said second article, any omission, defect, or mistake in the said second article, in any wise notwithstanding. . . .

15

Penal Law, 1703

This is one of a series of penal laws passed by the Irish Parliament under William III and Anne. This act was intended to disable the Catholic landowning class; in three-quarters of a century it had the effect of reducing their already limited share of Irish land by half, to an insignificant amount. The nature of other penal laws can be discerned in the acts repealing them (see no. 18).

Source: *Statutes at Large, Ireland*, IV: 12–31; 2 Anne, c.6.

An Act to prevent the further Growth of Popery

I. Whereas divers emissaries of the church of Rome, popish priests, and other persons of that perswasion, taking advantage of the weakness and ignorance of some of her Majesty's subjects, or of the extream sickness and decay of their reason and senses, in the absence of friends and spiritual guides, do daily endeavour to perswade and pervert them from the protestant religion, to the great dishonour of Almighty God, the weakening of the true religion, by His blessing so happily established in this realm, to the disquieting the peace and settlement, and discomfort of many particular families thereof; and in further manifestation of their hatred and aversion to the said true reli-

gion, many of the said persons, so professing the popish religion in this kingdom, have refused to make provision for their
own children for no other reason but their being of the protestant religion; and also have by cunning devices and contrivances
found out ways to avoid and elude the intents of an act of Parliament, made in the ninth year of the reign of the late King William the third for preventing protestants inter-marrying with
papists; and of several other laws made for the security of the
protestant religion; and whereas many persons so professing
the popish religion have it in their power to raise division among
protestants, by voting in elections for members of Parliament,
and also have it in their power to use other ways and means
tending to the destruction of their protestant interest in this kingdom; for remedy of which great mischiefs, and to prevent the
like evil practices for the future be it enacted . . . That if any
person or persons from and after the twenty-fourth day of March,
in this present year of our Lord 1703, shall seduce, perswade or
pervert any person or persons professing, or that shall profess,
the protestant religion, to renounce, forsake, or adjure the same,
and to profess the popish religion, or reconcile him or them to
the church of Rome, then and in such case every such person or
persons so seducing, as also every such protestant or protestants
who shall be so seduced, perverted and reconciled to popery,
shall for the said offences, being thereof lawfully convicted, incur the danger and penalty of premunire, mentioned in the stat-
ute of premunire made in England in the sixteenth year of the
reign of King Richard the second; and if any person or persons
professing the popish religion, shall from and after the said
twenty-fourth day of March send, or cause, or willingly suffer,
to be sent or conveyed any child under the age of one and twenty
years, except sailors, ship-boys, or the apprentice or factor of
some merchant in trade of merchandise, into France or any other

53

parts beyond the seas, out of her Majesty's dominions, without the special licence of her Majesty, her heirs or successors or of her or their chief governor or governors of this kingdom . . . he, she and they . . . shall incur the pains, penalties and forfeitures mentioned in an act made in the seventh year of his late Majesty King William, intituled, *An Act to restrain foreign education.* . . .

III. . . . in case the eldest son and heir of such popish parent shall be a protestant, that then from the time of inrolment in the high court of Chancery of a certificate of the bishop of the diocese, in which he shall inhabit, testifying his being a protestant, and conforming himself to the church of Ireland as by law established, such popish parent shall become, and shall be, only tenant for life of all the real estate, whereof such popish parent shall then be seized in fee-tail or fee-simple, and the reversion in fee shall be vested in such eldest son being a protestant; subject nevertheless to all such debts and realm incumbrances at the time of the inrolment of such certificate charging such estate, and subject also to such maintenances and portions for the other children, as well protestants as papists of such popish parents then born, or after to be born, as the said court of Chancery in manner aforesaid shall order. . . .

VI. And be it further enacted . . . That every papist, or person professing the popish religion, shall from and after the said twenty-fourth day of March be disabled, and is hereby made incapable, to buy and purchase either in his or in their own name, or in the name of any other person or persons to his or her use, or in trust for him or her, any manors, lands, tenements, or hereditaments, or any rents or profits out of the same, or any leases or terms thereof, other than any term of years not exceeding thirty-one years, whereon a rent not less than two-thirds of the improved yearly value, at the time of the making such leases of the tenements leased, shall be reserved. . . .

VII. And be it further enacted . . . That from and after the first day of February, in this present year of our Lord one thousand seven hundred and three, no papists, or person professing the popish religion, who shall not within six months after he or she shall become intituled to enter, or to take, or have the profits by descent, or by vertue of any devise or gift, or of any remainder already limited, or at any time hereafter to be limited, or by vertue of any trust of any lands, tenements or hereditaments, whereof any protestant now is, or hereafter shall be seized in fee-simple absolute, or fee-tail, or in such manner that after his death, or the death of him and his wife, the freehold is to come immediately to his son or sons, or issue in tail, if then of the age of eighteen years, or if under, within six months after he shall attain that age, until which time from his being so intituled he shall be under the care of such protestant relation or person conforming himself as aforesaid, as shall for that purpose be appointed by the high court of Chancery, for his being educated in the protestant religion, become a protestant, and conform himself to the church now established in this kingdom, shall take any benefit by reason of such descent, devise, gift, remainder, or trust, but from thenceforth during the life of such person, or until he or she do become a protestant, and conform as aforesaid, the nearest protestant relation or relations, or other protestant or protestants, and his and their heirs, being and continuing protestants, who shall or would be intituled to the same in case such person professing the popish religion, and not conforming as aforesaid, and all other intermediate popish relations and popish persons were actually dead, and his and their heirs shall have and enjoy the said lands. . . .

X. And be it further enacted . . . That all lands, any tenements and hereditaments, whereof any papist now is, or hereafter shall be, seized in fee-simple or fee-tail, shall from henceforth, so long as any papist shall be seized of or entitled to the same in fee-simple or fee-tail, be of the nature of gavelkind; and if not sold, aliened, or disposed of by such papist in his life time for good and valuable consideration of money really and *bona fide* paid for such estate, shall from such papist descend to, and be inherited by, all and every the sons of such papist any way inheritable to such estate, share and share alike, and not descend on or come to the eldest of such sons only, being a papist, as heir at law; and shall in like manner from such respective sons, being papists, descend to and be inherited by all and every the sons of such sons, share and share alike, and not descend to the eldest of such sons, being a papist, as heir at law only; and that for want of issue male of such papist, the same shall descend to all his daughters any way inheritable to such estate in equal proportions; and for want of such issue, among the collateral kindred of such papist, of the kin of his father, any way inheritable to such estate in equal degree; and for want of such kindred, to the collateral kindred of such papist of the kin of his mother, any way inheritable to such estate, and not otherwise. . . .

XII. Provided always, That if the eldest son or heir at law of such papist shall be a protestant at the time of the decease of such papist, . . . the lands, whereof such papist shall be so seized, shall descend to such eldest son or heir at law according to the rules of the common law of this realm, . . . and if the eldest son or heir at law of any such papist, who shall at the time of the decease of such papist, whose heir he is, be of the age of one and twenty years, shall become a protestant and conform himself to the church of Ireland, as by law established, within one year after such decease of such papist, or being then under the age of one and twenty years, shall within one year after he shall attain that age become a protestant, and conform himself as aforesaid, . . . he shall be intituled to, and shall have, and enjoy from thenceforth the whole real estate of such papist . . .

XVII. And be it further enacted . . . . That all and every person and persons, that shall be admitted, entered, placed, or taken into any office or offices, civil or military, or shall receive any pay, salary, fee, or wages belonging to or by reason of any office or place of trust, by reason of any patent or grant from her Majesty, or that shall have command or place of trust from or under her Majesty, or any of her predecessors or successors, or by her or their authority, or by authority derived from her or them, within this realm of Ireland, after the first day of Easter-term aforesaid, shall take the said oaths and repeat the said declaration, and subscribe the said oaths and declaration, in one of the said respective courts in the next term, or at the general quarter-session for that county, barony, or place, where he or they shall reside, next after his or their respective admittance or admittances into any such office . . . and all and every such person or persons so to be admitted as aforesaid, shall also receive the sacrament of the Lord's supper according to the usage of the church of Ireland, within three months after his or their admittance in or receiving their said authority and employments in some publick church, upon the Lord's-day commonly called Sunday, immediately after divine service and sermon, and every of the said respective persons, touching whom the said several provisions are here before made, in the respective court, where he or she takes the said oaths, shall first deliver a certificate of such his or her receiving the said sacrament as aforesaid, under the hands of the respective minister and church-wardens, and shall then make proof of the truth thereof of by two credible witnesses at the least, upon oath, all which shall be enquired of and put upon record in their respective courts. . . .

16

Irish Parliament Act, 1719

This act (also known as the Declaratory Act), passed in response to attempts by the Irish Parliament to assert some independence, is the fullest assertion by Great Britain of its authority over Ireland, though more symbolic than real. The "of right ought to be" clauses were repeated in the Declaratory Act passed for the American colonies in 1766, and (in negative form) supply the basis for the key sentence of the American Declaration of Independence.

Source: *Statutes at Large*, V, 179: 6 George I, c. 5.

An Act for the better securing the Dependency of the Kingdom of *Ireland* upon the Crown of *Great Britain*

I. Whereas the House of Lords of *Ireland* have of late, against Law, assumed to themselves a Power and Jurisdiction to examine, correct, and amend the Judgments and Decrees of the Courts of Justice in the Kingdom of *Ireland*; therefore for the better securing of the Dependency of *Ireland* upon the Crown of *Great Britain* . . . , be it declared by the King's most Excellent Majesty, by and with the Advice and Consent of the Lords Spiritual and Temporal, and Commons, in this present Parliament assembled . . . , That the said Kingdom of *Ireland* hath been, is, and of Right ought to be subordinate unto and dependent upon the

Imperial Crown of *Great Britain*, as being inseparably united and annexed thereunto; and that the King's Majesty, by and with the Advice and Consent of the Lords Spiritual and Temporal and Commons of *Great Britain* in Parliament assembled, had, hath, and of Right ought to have full Power and Authority to make Laws and Statutes of sufficient Force and Validity, to bind the Kingdom and People of *Ireland*.

II. And be it further declared and enacted. . . . That the House of Lords of Ireland have not, nor of Right ought to have any Jurisdiction to judge of, affirm, or reverse any Judgment, Sentence or Decree, given or made in any Court within the said Kingdom, and that all Proceedings before the said House of Lords upon any such Judgment, Sentence, or Decree, are, and are hereby declared to be utterly null and void to all Intents and Purposes whatsoever.

17

Repeal of the Declaratory Act, 1782

The repeal of the previous act and of Poynings' Law marked Grattan's successful campaign to restore the legislative independence of the Irish parliament.

Source: *Public General Statutes*, 22 Geo. III, 859–60.

An Act to repeal an Act, made in the Sixth Year of His late Majesty King *George* The First, intituled, *An Act for better securing the Dependency of the Kingdom of* Ireland *upon the Crown of* Great Britain

Whereas an Act was passed in the Sixth Year of the Reign of His late Majesty King *George* the First, intituled, *An Act for the better securing the Dependency of the Kingdom of* Ireland *upon the Crown of* Great Britain; . . . be it enacted. . . . That from and after the passing of this Act, the above-mentioned Act, and the several Matters and Things therein contained, shall be, and is and are hereby repealed.

18

Catholic Relief Acts, 1778, 1782, 1793

The first of these acts effectively repealed the penal law of 1703 (see above). The second repealed most of the other penal laws against Catholics, except as regarded political rights. The 1793 act, passed to avert the danger of revolution, gave qualified Catholics (not many at the time) the right to vote for members of Parliament and to hold minor offices, but excluded them from being elected to Parliament and from major offices. These exclusions framed the future issue of Catholic emancipation.

Source: *Statutes at Large, Ireland*, XI, 298–301, XII, 237–42, XVI, 685–92; 17–18 Geo. III c. 49; 21–22 Geo. III c. 24; 33 Geo. III c. 21.

An Act for the Relief of his Majesty's Subjects of this Kingdom professing the Popish Religion

Whereas by an act made in this kingdom in the second year of her late Majesty Queen Anne, entitled, *An act to prevent the further growth of popery*, and also by another act made in the eighth year of her said reign for explaining and amending the said act, the Roman Catholicks of Ireland are made subject to several disabilities and incapacities therein particularly mentioned; and whereas for their uniform peaceful behaviour for a long series of years it appears reasonable and expedient to relax the same, and it must tend not only to the cultivation and improvement of this kingdom, but to the prosperity and strength of all his Majesty's dominions, that his subjects of all denominations should enjoy the blessings of our free constitution, and should be bound to each other by mutual interest and mutual affection, therefore be it enacted. . . . That from and after the first day of August one thousand seven hundred and seventy eight it shall and may be lawful to and for any papist, or person professing the popish religion, subject to the provisoe hereinafter contained as to the taking and subscribing the oath and declaration therein mentioned, to take, hold, and enjoy any lease or leases for any term or term of years, not exceeding nine hundred and ninety-nine years certain or for any term of years determinable upon any number of lives, not exceeding five . . . as any other his Majesty's subjects in this kingdom, and the same to dispose of by will or otherwise as he shall think fit; and all lands tenements, and hereditaments, whereof any papist or person professing the popish religion is now seized or shall be seized by virtue of a title legally derived by, from, or under such person or persons, now seized in fee simple or fee tail, whether at law or in equity, shall from and after the time aforesaid be descendable, deviseable, and transferable, as fully, beneficially, and effectually, as if the same were in the seizin of any other of his Majesty's subjects in this kingdom. . . .

VI. And whereas by an act made in this kingdom in the second year of the reign of her late Majesty Queen Anne, entitled, *An act to prevent the further growth of popery*, it is amongst other things enacted to the effect following; in case the eldest son and heir of a popish parent shall be a protestant, . . . such popish parent shall become and be only tenant for life of all the real estate, whereof such popish parent shall then be seized in fee tail or fee simple, and the reversion in fee shall be vested in such eldest son, being a protestant subject, . . . and whereas it is found inexpedient to continue any longer that part of the said recited act: be it enacted . . . That from and after the first day of November one thousand seven hundred and seventy eight the conformity of the eldest son . . . shall not affect or alter the estate of any popish parent . . . but such popish parent shall remain seized and possessed of the same estate and interest in all and every his or her real estate, as he or she would have been, if such eldest son had not conformed, or the said act of the second of Queen Anne had not been made. . . .

An Act for the further Relief of His Majesty's Subjects of this Kingdom professing the Popish Religion

I. Whereas all such of his Majesty's subjects in this kingdom, of whatever persuasion, as have heretofore taken and subscribed, or shall hereafter take and subscribe, the oath of allegiance and declaration prescribed by an act passed in the thirteenth and fourteenth years of his present Majesty's reign, entitled, *An act to enable his Majesty's subjects of whatever persuasion, to testify their allegiance to him;* ought to be considered as good and loyal subjects to his Majesty, his crown and government: and whereas a continuance of several of the laws formerly enacted, and still in force in this kingdom, against persons professing the popish religion, is therefore unnecessary, in respect to those who have taken or shall take the said oath, and is injurious to the real welfare and prosperity of Ireland; therefore be it enacted . . . That from and after the first day of May, one thousand seven hundred and eighty two it shall and may be lawful to and for any person or persons professing the popish religion, to purchase, or take by grant, limitation, descent, or devise, any lands, tenements, or hereditaments in this kingdom, or any interest therein (except advowsons, and also except any manor or borough, or any part of a manor or borough, the freeholders or inhabitants whereof are intitled to vote for the burgesses to represent such borough or manor in parliament) and the same to dispose of as he, she, or they shall think fit, . . .

V. And be it enacted. . . . That no popish ecclesiastick, who hath heretofore taken and subscribed, or who shall hereafter take and subscribe, the oath of allegiance and declaration, prescribed by an act passed in the thirteenth and fourteenth years of his present majesty's reign, intituled, *An act to enable his Majesty's subjects of whatever persuasion, to testify their allegiance to him*, in the manner and form as herein after is particularly specified and set forth, and who shall register his christian and sirnames, place of abode, age, and parish, if he have a parish, and the time and place of his receiving his first, and every other popish orders, and from whom he received them, with the register of the diocese where his place of abode is (for every which registry the sum of one shilling and no more shall be paid to the register) shall, after the passing of this act, be subject to any of the penalties, incapacities, or disabilities, mentioned in an act made in the ninth year of the reign of King William the third, intituled, *An act for banishing all popish papists exercising any ecclesiastical jurisdiction, and regulars of the popish clergy out of this kingdom*, or in an act made in the second year of Queen Ann, intituled, *An act for registering the popish clergy*, or in an act made in the second year of Queen Ann, intituled, *An act to prevent the further growth of popery*, or in an act made in the second year of Queen Ann, intituled, *An act to prevent popish priests from coming into this kingdom*, or in an act made in the fourth year of Queen Ann, intituled, *An act to explain and amend an act entitled, An act for registering popish clergy*; or in an act made in the eighth year of Queen Ann, intituled, *An act for explaining and amending an act, entitled, An act to prevent the further growth of popery.* . . .

XII. And be it enacted . . . That so much of an act passed in the seventh year of King William the third, intituled, *An act for the better securing the government by disarming papists*, as subjects any papist, who shall after the twentieth day of January, one thousand six hundred and ninety five have or keep in his possession, or in the possession of any other person to his use or at his disposal, any horse, gelding, or mare, which shall be of the value of five pounds or more, to the penalties therein mentioned; and also so much of an act passed in the eighth year of Queen Anne, intituled, *An act for explaining and amending an act, intituled, An act to prevent the further growth of popery*, as enables the lord lieutenant or other chief governors of this kingdom, to seize and secure any horse, mare or gelding belonging to any papist, or reputed papist, upon any invasion likely to happen, or in case of intestine war broke out, or likely to break out, shall be, and is, and are hereby repealed. . . .

An Act for the Relief of His Majesty's Popish, or Roman Catholick Subjects of Ireland

Whereas various acts of parliament have been passed, imposing on his Majesty's subjects professing the popish or Roman catholick religion, many restraints and disabilities, to which other subjects of this realm are not liable, and from the peaceful and loyal demeanour of his majesty's popish or Roman Catholick subjects, it is fit that such restraints and disabilities shall be discontinued: Be it therefore enacted . . . That his Majesty's subjects being papists, or persons professing the popish or Roman catholick religion, or married to papists, or persons professing the popish or Roman catholick religion, or educating any of their children in that religion, shall not be liable or subject to any penalties, forfeitures, disabilities, or incapacities, or to any laws for the limitation, charging, or discovering of their estates and property, real or personal, or touching the acquiring of property, or securities affecting property, save such as his Majesty's subjects of the protestant religion are liable and subject to; and that such parts of all oaths as are required to be taken by persons in order to qualify themselves for voting at elections for members to serve in parliament; . . . as import to deny that the person taking the same is a papist or married to a papist, or educates his children in the popish religion, shall not hereafter be required to be taken by any voter, but shall be omitted by the person administering the same; and that it shall not be necessary, in order to entitle a papist, or person professing the popish or Roman catholick religion to vote at an election of members to serve in parliament, that he should at, or previous to his voting, take the oaths of allegiance and abjuration. . . .

VII. And be it enacted, That it shall and may be lawful for papists, or persons professing the popish or Roman catholick religion, to hold, exercise, and enjoy all civil and military offices, or places of trust or profit under his majesty, his heirs and successors, in this kingdom . . . provided that every such person shall take and subscribe the oath appointed by the said act passed in the thirteenth and fourteenth years of his Majesty's reign, entitled, *An act to enable his majesty's subjects of whatever persuasion to testify their allegiance to him*; and also the oath and declaration following, that is to say,

I A.B. do hereby declare, that I do profess the Roman catholick religion. I A.B. do swear, that I do abjure, condemn, and detest, as unchristian and impious, the principle that it is lawful to murder, destroy, or any ways injure any person whatsoever, for or under the pretence of being a heretick; and I do declare solemnly before God, that I believe, that no act in itself unjust, immoral, or wicked, can ever be justified or excused by, or under pretence or colour, that it was done either for the good of the church, or in obedience to any ecclesiastical power whatsoever. I also declare, that it is not an article of the catholick faith, neither am I thereby required to believe or profess that the pope is infallible, or that I am bound to obey any order in its own nature immoral, though the pope or any ecclesiastical power should issue or direct such order, but on the contrary, I hold that it would be sinful in me to pay any respect or obedience thereto; I further declare, that I do not believe that any sin whatsoever, committed by me, can be forgiven at the mere will of any pope, or of any priest, or of any person or persons whatsoever, but that sincere sorrow for past sins, a firm and sincere resolution to avoid future guilt, and to atone to God, are previous and indispensable requisites to establish a well-founded expectation of forgiveness; and that any person who receives absolution without these previous requisites, so far from obtaining thereby any remission of his sins, incurs the additional guilt of violating a sacrament; and I do swear that I will defend to the utmost of my power the settlement and arrangement of property in this country, as established by the laws now in being; I do hereby disclaim, disavow and solemnly abjure any intention to subvert the present church establishment, for the purpose of substituting a catholick establishment in its stead; and I do solemnly swear, that I will not exercise any privilege to which I am or may become entitled, to disturb and weaken the protestant religion and protestant government in this kingdom.

So help me God. . . .

IX. Provided always, and be it enacted, that nothing herein contained shall extend, or be construed to extend to enable any person to sit or vote in either house of parliament, or to hold, exercise, or enjoy the office of lord lieutenant, lord deputy, or other chief governor of this kingdom, lord high chancellor or keeper, or commissioner of the great seal of this kingdom, lord high treasurer, chancellor of the exchequer, justice of the court of king's-bench, or common pleas, baron of the court of exchequer, judge of the high court of admiralty, master or keeper of the rolls, secretary, vice-treasurer, teller and cashier of the exchequer, or auditor-general, lieutenant or governor, or custos rotulorum of counties, secretary to the lord lieutenant, lord deputy, or other chief governor or governors of this kingdom, member of his majesty's most honourable privy council, prime serjeant, attorney-general, solicitor-general, second and third serjeants-at-law, or king's counsel, masters in chancery, provost, or fellow of the college of the holy and undivided Trinity of queen Elizabeth, near Dublin, postmaster-general, master and lieutenant-general of his Majesty's ordnance, commander-in-chief of his Majesty's forces, generals on the staff, and sheriffs and sub-sheriffs of any county in this kingdom or any office contrary to the rules, orders and directions made and established by the lord lieutenant and council, in pursuance of the act passed in the seventeenth and eighteenth years of the reign of king Charles the second, entitled, *An act for the explaining of some doubts arising upon an act*, entitled, *An act for the better execution of his Majesty's gracious declaration for the settlement of his kingdom of Ireland*, . . . unless he shall have taken, made, and subscribed the oaths, and declaration, and performed the several requisites which by any law heretofore made, and now of force, are required to enable any person to sit or vote, or to hold, exercise, and enjoy the said offices respectively. . . .

19

The United Irishmen (1791)

This declaration was first drawn up by the Dublin Society of United Irishmen in 1791; a peaceable political document, it stands as a monument of modern secular nationalism. It was later expanded on a national basis in 1797, by which time the organization had shifted towards revolutionary means.

Source: Curtis and McDowell, 238–39 (see document 4).

In the present era of reform, when unjust governments are falling in every quarter of Europe, when religious persecution is compelled to abjure her tyranny over conscience, when the rights of men are ascertained in theory, and that theory substantiated by practice, when antiquity can no longer defend absurd and oppressive forms, against the common sense and common interests of mankind, when all governments are acknowledged to originate from the people, and to be so far only obligatory, as they protect their rights, and promote their welfare, we think it our duty, as Irishmen, to come forward, and state what we feel to be our heavy grievance, and what we know to be its effectual remedy. We have no national government, we are ruled by Englishmen, and the servants of Englishmen, whose object is the interest of another country, whose instrument is corruption, and whose strength is the weakness of Ireland; and these men have the whole of the power and patronage of the country, as mean to seduce and subdue the honesty of her representatives in the legislature. Such an extrinsic power, acting with uniform force, in a direction too frequently opposite to the true line of our obvious interest, can be resisted with effect solely by unanimity, decision, and spirit in the people, qualities which may be exerted most legally, constitutionally, and efficaciously, by that great measure, essential to the prosperity and freedom of Ireland, an equal representation of all the people in parliament.

Impressed with these sentiments, we have agreed to form an association, to be called the Society of United Irishmen, and we do pledge ourselves to our country, and mutually to each other, that we will steadily support, and endeavour by all due means to carry into effect the following resolutions:

1st. Resolved, That the weight of English influence in the government of this country is so great, as to require a cordial union among all the people of Ireland, to maintain that balance which is essential to the preservation of our liberties, and extension of our commerce.

2nd. That the sole constitutional mode by which this influence can be opposed is by a complete and radical reform of the representation of the people in parliament.

3rd .That no reform is practicable, efficacious, or just, which shall not include Irishmen of every religious persuasion.

Satisfied, as we are, that the intestine divisions among Irishmen have too often given encouragement and impunity to profligate, audacious, and corrupt administrations, in measures which, but for these divisions, they durst not have attempted, we submit our resolutions to the nation, as the basis of our political faith. We have gone to what we conceived to be the root of the evil. We have stated what we conceive to be remedy. With a parliament thus formed, everything is easy—without it, nothing can be done—and we do call on, and most earnestly exhort our countrymen in general to follow our example, and to form similar societies in every quarter of the kingdom, for the promotion of constitutional knowledge, the abolition of bigotry in religion and politics, and the equal distribution of the rights of man throughout all sects and denominations of Irishmen. . . .

20

Act of Union, 1800

This is the British text of the identical Articles of Union passed by the two parliaments of Great Britain and Ireland. The result was to end the separate political identity of Ireland.

Source: *Statutes at Large*, XIV, 359–75: 40 Geo. III, c. 67.

An Act for the Union of Great Britain and Ireland

Whereas, in pursuance of his Majesty's . . . Recommendation to the two Houses of Parliament in *Great Britain* and *Ireland* respectively . . . , the two Houses of the Parliament of *Great Britain* and the two Houses of the Parliament of *Ireland* have severally agreed and resolved, that . . . it will be advisable to concur in such Measures as may best tend to unite the two Kingdoms of *Great Britain* and *Ireland* into one Kingdom. . . . And whereas, in furtherance of the said Resolution, both Houses of the said two Parliaments respectively have likewise agreed upon certain Articles for effectuating and establishing the said Purposes, in the Tenor following:

ARTICLE FIRST
. . . that the said Kingdoms of *Great Britain* and *Ireland* shall . . . be united into one Kingdom, by the name of the *United Kingdom* of *Great Britain* and *Ireland*. . . .

ARTICLE SECOND
... that the Succession to the Imperial Crown of the said United Kingdom, and of the Dominions thereunto belonging, shall continue limited and settled ... according to the existing Laws, and to the Terms of Union between England and Scotland.

ARTICLE THIRD
... that the said United Kingdom be represented in one and the same Parliament. ...

ARTICLE FOURTH
... that four Lords Spiritual of *Ireland* by Rotation of Sessions, and twenty-eight Lords Temporal of *Ireland,* elected for Life by the Peers of *Ireland,* shall be the Number to sit and vote on the Part of *Ireland* in the House of Lords of the Parliament of the United Kingdom; and one hundred Commoners (two for each County of *Ireland*, two for the City of *Dublin*, two for the City of *Cork*, one for the University of *Trinity College*, and one for each of the thirty-one most considerable Cities, Towns, and Boroughs), be the Number to sit and vote on the Part of *Ireland* in the House of Commons of the Parliament of the United Kingdom. ...

ARTICLE FIFTH
... That the *Churches* of *England* and *Ireland*, as now by Law established, be united into one Protestant Episcopal Church, to be called, The *United Church of England and Ireland*; and that the Doctrine, Worship, Discipline, and Government of the said United Church shall be, and shall remain in full force forever, as the same are now by Law established for the Church of *England;* and that the Continuance and Preservation of the said United Church, as the established Church of *England* and *Ire-*

73

land, shall be deemed and taken to be an essential and fundamental Part of the Union. . . .

ARTICLE SIXTH

. . . That his Majesty's Subjects of *Great Britain* and *Ireland* shall . . . be entitled to the same Privileges . . . as to Encouragements and Bounties on the like Articles, being the Growth, Produce, or Manufacture of either Country respectively, and generally in respect of Trade and Navigation in all Ports and Places in the United Kingdom and its Dependencies. . . .

ARTICLE EIGHTH

. . . That all Laws in force at the Time of the Union, and all the Courts of Civil and Ecclesiastical Jurisdiction within the respective Kingdoms, shall remain as now by Law established within the same; subject only to such Alterations and Regulations from Time to Time as circumstances may appear to the Parliament of the United Kingdom to require; provided that all Writs of Error and Appeals depending at the Time of the Union or hereafter to be brought, and which might now be finally decided by the House of Lords of either Kingdom, shall, from and after the union, be finally decided by the House of Lords of the United Kingdom. . . .

. . . be it enacted . . . That, the said . . . Articles . . . be ratified, confirmed, and approved . . . , and they are hereby declared to be the Articles of the Union of *Great Britain* and *Ireland*; and the same shall be in force and have effect forever, from the first Day of *January* which shall be in the Year of our Lord one thousand eight hundred one, provided that before that Period an Act shall have been passed by the Parliament of *Ireland* for carrying into effect, in the like Manner, the said . . . articles. . . .

21

Robert Emmet: Speech from the Dock (1803)

In English law, a convicted prisoner is allowed to speak from the "dock" which encloses him to give reasons why sentence of death should not be passed on him. Emmet creatively took this as an opportunity to justify himself and his cause. Others followed his example, thereby creating a new genre of oratory—unfortunately, a terminal genre.

Source: Alan O'Day and John Stevenson, eds., *Irish Historical Documents Since 1800* (Dublin: Gill and Macmillan, 1992), 15–16; from Richard R. Madden, *The United Irishmen, Their Lives and Times* (4 vols., 1842–46; Dublin, 1857–60), 114–15.

My lords, as to why judgment of death and execution should not be passed upon me according to law I have nothing to say; but as to why my character should not be relieved from the imputations and calumnies thrown out against it I have much to say. . . Whilst the man dies, his memory lives; and that mine may not forfeit all claim to the respect of my countrymen, I seize upon this opportunity to vindicate myself from some of the charges alleged against me.

. . . My object, and that of the rest of the Provisional Government was to effect a total separation between Great Britain and

Ireland—to make Ireland totally independent of Great Britain, but not to let her become a dependent of France.

... I have but a few words more to say—my ministry is now ended. I am going to my cold and silent grave; my lamp of life is nearly extinguished. I have parted with everything that was dear to me in this life for my country's cause, and abandoned another idol I adored in my heart—the object of my affections. My race is run—the grave opens to receive me, and I sink into its bosom. I am ready to die—I have not been allowed to vindicate my character. I have but one request to ask at my departure from this world—it is *the charity of its silence*. Let no man write my epitaph; for as no man who knows my motives dare now vindicate them, let not prejudice or ignorance asperse them. Let them rest in obscurity and peace: my memory be left in oblivion, and my tomb remain uninscribed, until other times and other men can do justice to my character. When my country takes her place among the nations of the earth, then, and not till then, let my epitaph be written. I have done.

22

Roman Catholic
Emancipation Act, 1829

This act somewhat grudgingly conceded Catholic Emancipation. The oath
renounces Jacobitism and other political offences by Catholics since the
time of Elizabeth; it is actually no worse than the oaths which had been
attached to various Catholic Relief Acts since 1774.
Source: *Public General Statutes*, LXV, 105–16; 10 Geo. IV, c. 7.

An Act for the Relief of His Majesty's Roman
Catholic Subjects

Whereas by various Acts of Parliament certain Restraints and
Disabilities are imposed on the Roman Catholic Subjects of
His Majesty to which other Subjects of His Majesty are not
liable: . . . and whereas by various Acts certain Oaths and certain Declarations . . . are or may be required to be taken, made,
and subscribed by the Subjects of His Majesty, as Qualifica-
tions for sitting and voting in Parliament, and for the Enjoyment of certain Offices, Franchises, and Civil Rights: Be it
enacted . . . That from and after the Commencement of this
Act all such Parts of the said Acts as require the said Declara-

tions . . . as a Qualification for sitting and voting in Parliament, or for the Exercise or Enjoyment of any Office, Franchise, or Civil Right, be and the same are (save as herein-after provided and excepted) hereby repealed.

II. And be it enacted, That from and after the Commencement of this Act, it shall be lawful for any Person professing the Roman Catholic Religion, being a Peer, or who shall after the Commencement of this Act be returned as a Member of the House of Commons, to sit and vote in either House of Parliament respectively, being in all other respects duly qualified to sit and vote therein, upon taking and subscribing the following oath, instead of the Oaths of Allegiance, Supremacy, and Abjuration:

'I A.B. do sincerely promise and swear, That I will be faithful and bear true Allegiance to His Majesty King *George* the Fourth and will defend him to the utmost of my Power against all Conspiracies and Attempts whatever which shall be made against his Person, Crown, or Dignity; . . . And I do faithfully promise to maintain, support, and defend, to the utmost of my Power, the Succession of the Crown, which . . . stands limited to the Princess *Sophia*, Electress of *Hanover*, and the Heirs of her Body, being Protestants, hereby utterly renouncing and abjuring any Obedience or Allegiance unto any other Person claiming or pretending a Right to the Crown of this Realm: And I do further declare, that it is not an Article of my Faith, and that I do denounce, reject, and abjure the Opinion, that Princes excommunicated or deprived by the Pope, or any other Authority of the See of *Rome*, may be deposed or murdered by their Subjects or by any Person whatsoever: And I do declare that I do not believe that the Pope of *Rome,* or any other foreign Prince, Prelate, Person, State, or Potentate, hath or ought to have any Temporal or Civil Jurisdiction, Power, Superiority, or Pre-eminence, directly or indirectly, within this Realm. I do swear, That I will defend to the utmost of my Power the Settlement of Property within this Realm, as established by the Laws: And I do hereby disclaim, disavow, and solemnly abjure any Intention to subvert the present Church Establishment as settled by Law within this Realm: And I do solemnly swear, That I will never exercise any Privilege to which I am or may become entitled, to disturb or weaken the Protestant Religion or Protestant Government in the United Kingdom. . . . So help me GOD.'

V. And be it further enacted, That it shall be lawful for Persons professing the Roman Catholic Religion to vote at elections of Members to serve in Parliament for *England* and for *Ireland*, and also to vote at the Elections of Representative Peers of *Scotland* and of *Ireland,* and to be elected such Representative Peers, being in all other respects duly qualified, upon taking and subscribing the Oath herein-before appointed. . . .

23

Alexis de Tocqueville: Journey in Ireland (1835)

The French political writer Alexis de Tocqueville, famous for his *Democracy in America*, also travelled in England and Ireland, keeping diaries. The first extract from his Irish travels (July–August 1835) is a brief description of the wretched living conditions of the peasants; it is typical of many such passages in eighteenth- and nineteenth-century writing and is included as an example of that genre. The larger portion describes his interview with William Kinsella, bishop of Ossory, at Kilkenny. The bishop was a shrewd if biased commentator, and de Tocqueville was a shrewd listener; as he said of another interview: "It is above all necessary to consider this conversation (as all the others) as indicating the state of feelings more than the naked truth" (39).

Source: *Alexis de Tocqueville's Journey in Ireland July-August, 1835*, tr. and ed. Emmet Larkin (Washington: The Catholic University of America Press, 1990), 39, 59, 61–64.

Most of the dwellings of the country very poor looking. A very large number of them wretched to the last degree. Walls of mud, roofs of thatch, one room. No chimney, smoke goes out the door. The pig lies in the middle of the house. It is Sunday. Yet the population looks very wretched. Many wear clothes with holes or much patched. Most of them are bare-headed and barefoot.

19 July 1835

We went to see today (24 July 1835) Msgr. Kinsely, bishop of Kilkenny. We found him very simply lodged. He told us:

My revenue is not large and still less fixed. I have only what comes to me by the voluntary gifts of the faithful, but I can sometimes give a dinner. I have a gig and a horse. I find myself rich enough and I would despair if the state wished to pay me. Last spring I went to London for the sole purpose of preventing such a measure from being proposed. It would break the union that now exists between the clergy and the people. Now the people regard us as their own work and are attached to us because of what they give us. If we received money from the state they would regard us as public officials, and when we should advise them to respect law and order, they would say, they are paid for that. . . .

Msgr. Kinseley is a very likeable man, very spiritual, perspicacious, and having enough sense to be impartial (as far as an Irishman can be) and finding pleasure in showing it. There prevails in his language a certain note of triumph, which indicates the head of a party who arrives in power after having been oppressed for a long time. I believe that he is very sincere in wishing that the church should not be part of the state, but I wonder if he does not think, at bottom, that the state would do well enough as part of the church. These are nuances. I am perhaps mistaken.

Q. I have often heard it said in England and even in Ireland that the Catholic population was half savage? The charge is probably false.

A. I am obliged to say it is true in part. But whose fault is it, if not those who have reduced them to this state by their bad government? What became of the Greeks under the Turks? Before 1792 we were not able to have schools, we were not able to be called to the bar, the magistracy was closed to us. We were not able to possess land. . . Examine the laws of that period [and] you will be frightened. Now, I confess that the population has some of the characteristics and unhappily the defects of savage peoples. These people have all the divine virtues. They have the faith. No one is a better Christian than the Irishman. Their morals are pure. Their crimes are very rarely premeditated. But they lack essentially the civil virtues. They are without foresight, without prudence. Their courage is instinctive. They throw themselves at an obstacle with extraordinary violence and if they are not successful at the first attempt, they tire of it. They are changeable, love excitement, combat. . . .

Q. Is the memory of the confiscations still alive?

A. Yes, as a vague instinct of hatred against the conquerors. There are still in a great many places families who are known to have been dispossessed. . . .

Q. What is, in your opinion, the principle cause of the poverty of the country?

A. A too-numerous population. It is certain that the land divided up, or rather not divided up, as it is in Ireland, cannot furnish a constant employment for our population. I believe that the consequences of absenteeism are exaggerated. It does harm but I regard it above all as a troublesome sign of the separation that exists between the different classes.

Q. Do you think that a poor law is necessary?

A. Yes, I believe so without hesitation. It would have, among other things, this result. Today, not only is there a shortage of land, but many estates have been converted into grasslands; those where 150 laborers would be found, ten shepherds suffice. If there were a tax on estates, the owners of these grasslands would find that they gained little by disposing of the land in this way; for if the land thus yielded more, and the landlord were obliged by the poor law to give all or part of his surplus in order to feed those whom he prevents from subsisting, he would restore his grasslands to wheat, or at the very least, he would no longer put the wheat to grassland.

Q. It is said that there are in Ireland now huge amounts of uncultivated land, which could be cultivated?

A. Yes. But up to the present, the farmer has been little disposed to invest in clearing land. Hardly was the land cultivated than the tithe collector and the state tax collector would appear.

Q. You have told me that morals were pure?

A. Extremely pure. Twenty years in the confessional have made me aware that the misconduct of girls is very rare, and that of married women almost unknown. Public opinion, one might almost say, goes too far in this direction. A woman *suspected* is lost for life. . . . Suicide is unknown. It is nearly unknown in the towns and still less in the country that a Catholic fails to make his Easter communion.

I say again that they have the divine virtues, but they are ignorant, violent, intemperate, and incapable as savages of resisting the first impulse. . . .

Q. Is it true that the Protestant aristocracy is very much in debt?

A. Yes. Nothing is more true. Most of them sink under their burden. Everyday we see the rich Catholics of the towns lend money to Protestants, and these latter end by being obliged to break *entail* and sell their lands. In this way many of the estates pass gradually into the hands of Catholics. . . .

24

Daniel O'Connell: Speech at Mullingar, May 14, 1843

This speech at the height of the Repeal campaign is a good example of
O'Connell's oratory, a genial demagoguery, and his nationalism, democratic and constitutional.

Source: *The Nation*, May 20, 1843, 498–99.

My first object is to get Ireland for the Irish (loud cheers). I am
content that the English should have England, but they have had
the domination of this country too long, and it is time that the
Irish should at length get their own country—that they should
get the management of their own country—the regulation of
their own country —the enjoyment of their own country—that
the Irish should have Ireland (great cheers). Nobody can know
how to govern us as well as we would know how to do it ourselves—nobody could know how to relieve our wants as well as
we would ourselves—nobody could have so deep an interest in
our prosperity, or could be so well fitted for remedying our evils,
and procuring happiness for us as we would ourselves (hear,
hear). . . . What numberless advantages would not the Irish enjoy if they possessed their own country? A domestic parliament

would encourage Irish manufactures. The linen trade, and the woollen would be spreading amongst you. An Irish parliament would foster Irish commerce, and protect Irish agriculture. The labourer, the artizan, and the shopkeeper would be all benefited by the repeal of the union. . . . I ask did you ever hear of the tithe rent charge (groans). Are you satisfied to be paying parsons who do not pray for you (no, no). It is time, therefore, that they should be put an end to (hear, hear). . . . I next want to get rid of the poor rates (cheers). England does charity in the way a person will throw a bone to a dog, by slashing it in between its teeth (hear, hear). That is the poor law charity, the charity of the commissioners and assistant-commissioners, and all concerned under them except the poor themselves, and when they do give relief they take up the poor as if they were criminals, or as if poverty were a crime to be punished by perpetual imprisonment (hear and cheers). . . . Would I not have the tithe rent-charge and the ecclesiastical revenues to apply for their relief? And would I not with their aid be able to maintain hospitals for the sick, the lame, the impotent, the aged, and all those who are real objects of charity, and for whom the doors would be open at every hour of the day and during a part of the night, so that anybody who did not like to remain might go out when they liked (hear, hear, and cheers)? I would thus do you two pieces of service by the repeal of the Union. I would relieve the poor without the imposition of poor rates, and I would prevent you from paying any clergy but your own (loud cheers). . . . Give me the repeal, and the national treasury will pay for the making and repairing of all the roads, bridges, and public buildings; and instead of the poor farmers and occupiers paying the money themselves, it will come from the treasury, and would go in giving employment to those who now have to pay it (hear, hear). I will tell you another thing I want to do. I want that every head of a family, every married man and every householder should have a right to vote for members of parliament. . . . I would institute the ballot-box. Every married man should have a vote, and any blackguard who could not get a wife anywhere I would not pity him to be without the vote (cheer and laughter). . . . You know that the landlords have duties as well as rights, and I would establish the fixity of tenure (loud cheers) to remind them of these duties. . . . They say we want separation from England, but what I want is to prevent separation taking place, and there is not a man in existence more loyally attached than I am to the Queen—God bless her. The present state of Ireland is nearly unendurable, and if the people of Ireland had not some person like me to lead them in the paths of peace and constitutional exertion, I am afraid of the result (hear). While I live I will stand by the throne (hear, hear). But what motive could we have to separate if we obtain all those blessings and advantages I have been enumerating? They would all serve as solid golden links of connexion with England. But I would be glad to know what good did the Union do (hear, hear)? What I want you to do is, for every one of you to join me in looking for Repeal. As many of you as are willing to do so let them hold up their hands [here every person in the immense assemblage raised his hands aloft amidst loud and continued cheers]. I see you have ready hands, and I know you have stout hearts too. But what do I want you to do? Is it to turn out into battle or war (cries of no, no)? Is it to commit riot or crime (cries of no, no)? Remember 'whoever commits a crime gives strength to the enemy' (hear, hear, and cheers). . . . I want you to do nothing that is not open and legal, but if the people unite with me and follow my advice it is impossible not to get the Repeal (loud cheers and cries of 'we will'). . . . But nothing could be more true, that there was no pursuit of Roman catholic interests as opposed to protestant, and that the object in view was to benefit the whole nation; and because it was a national movement it should never be abandoned until justice was done to the nation (loud cheers). Even their enemies should admit the progress they had made; and let him have but three millions of Repealers, and then he would make his arrangements for obtaining Repeal. He would have the Repealers send up three hundred gentlemen, chosen from various parts of the country, each entrusted with £100, that would be £30,000. They should meet in Dublin to consult upon the best means of obtaining legislative independence. They would not leave Dublin till they would agree to an act of parliament to establish a domestic legislature, household suffrage, vote by ballot, fixity of tenure, and a law against absentees having estates in the country. Many estates would then be sold, in lots and purchased by those who would become small proprietors. . . .

25

Thomas Francis Meagher: Speech, July 28, 1846

The split of the Young Irelanders from O'Connell's Repeal movement was precipitated by an O'Connellite motion in the Repeal Association to condemn the use of physical force absolutely. Meagher stated the Young Ireland position (at that date only theoretical) that physical force may be used when necessary.

Source: *The Nation*, August 1, 1846, 667.

I do advocate the peaceful policy of this association (Cheers). It is the only policy we can and should adopt (Cheers). If that policy be pursued with truth, with courage, with stern determination of purpose, I do firmly believe that it will succeed (Loud and enthusiastic cheers). But, my lord, I dissented from the resolutions in question for other reasons (Hear, hear). . . . I dissented from these resolutions, for I felt that by assenting to them I should have pledged myself to the unqualified repudiation of physical force in all countries, at all times, and in every circumstance. This I could not do, for my lord, I do not abhor the use of arms in the vindication of national rights (Cheers). There are times when arms will alone suffice, and when political ameliorations call for a drop of blood—(cheers) and many thousand drops of blood (Enthusiastic cheering and cries of oh, oh). Opinion I admit will operate against opinion. But, as the hon. Member for Kilkenny observed, force must be used against force (Cheers, and some confusion). The soldier is proof against an argument but he is not proof against a bullet. The man that will listen to reason, let him be reasoned with, but it is the weaponed arm of the patriot that can alone avail against battalioned despotism (Loud cheers). Then, my lord, I do not disclaim the use of force as immoral, nor do I believe that it is the truth to say that the God of Heaven withholds his sanction from the use of arms. . . . His Almighty hand has ever been stretched forth from His throne of light, to consecrate the flag of freedom, to bless the patriot's sword (Loud and enthusiastic cheering). Be it for the defence or be it for the assertion of a nation's liberty, I look upon the sword as a sacred weapon (No, no, from the Rev. Mr. Hopkins). And if my lord it has sometimes reddened the shroud of the oppressor, like the annointed rod of the high priest, it has at other times blossomed into flowers to deck the freeman's brow (Vehement applause). Abhor the sword and stigmatize the sword? No, my lord, for in the cragged passes of the Tyrol it cut in pieces the banner of the Bavarian, and won an immortality for the peasant of Innsbruck (Hear). Abhor the sword and stigmatize the sword? No, my lord, for at its blow a giant nation sprung up from the waters of the far Atlantic, and by its redeeming magic the fettered colony became a daring free republic. Abhor the sword and stigmatize the sword? No, my lord, for it scourged the Dutch marauders out of the fine old towns of Belgium, back into their own phlegmatic swamps—(cheers)—and knocked their flag, and laws, and sceptre, and bayonets, into the sluggish waters of the Scheldt (Enthusiastic cheers).

26

Fenian Oath (1859)

The Irish Republican Brotherhood, known as the Fenians, was founded in 1858. The oath was redrafted by James Stephens in 1859 to remove references to a secret society, which offended the Catholic clergy. It was in fact a secret society; the text of the oath had to be reconstructed from memory.
Source: John O'Leary, *Recollections of Fenians and Fenianism* (London, 1896), I, 121.

I, A.B., in the presence of Almighty God, do solemnly swear allegiance to the Irish Republic, now virtually established; and that I will do my utmost, at every risk, while life lasts, to defend its independence and integrity; and finally, that I will yield implicit obedience in all things, not contrary to the laws of God, to the commands of my superior officers. So help me God! Amen.

27

"God Save Ireland" (1868)

The abortive Fenian risings of 1867 were followed by a jailbreak in Manchester, England, in which a police constable was killed. English law regarded this as murder, and three men were hanged, dying with the words "God save Ireland." The "Manchester martyrs" were commemorated in 1868 with this song, which became a battle hymn of Irish nationalism, best sung in pubs.

Source: T.D. Sullivan, *Songs and Poems* (Dublin, 1899), 14–15.

GOD SAVE IRELAND

Air—"Tramp, Tramp, the Boys are Marching."

I.

High upon the gallows tree
Swung the noble-hearted Three
By the vengeful tyrant stricken in their bloom;
But they met him face to face,
With the courage of their race,
And they went with souls undaunted to their doom.
"God save Ireland!" said the heroes;

"God save Ireland!" said they all:
"Whether on the scaffold high
"Or the battle-field we die,
"Oh, what matter, when for Erin dear we fall!"

II.

Girt around with cruel foes,
Still their spirit proudly rose,
For they thought of hearts that loved them, far and
near;
Of the millions true and brave
O'er the ocean's swelling wave,
And the friends in holy Ireland ever dear.
"God save Ireland!" said they proudly;
"God save Ireland!" said they all:
"Whether on the scaffold high
"Or the battle-field we die,
"Oh, what matter, when for Erin dear we fall!"

III.

Climbed they up the rugged stair,
Rang their voices out in prayer,
Then with England's fatal cord around them cast,
Close beneath the gallows tree,
Kissed like brothers lovingly,
True to home and faith and freedom to the last.
"God save Ireland!" prayed they loudly;
"God save Ireland!" said they all:
"Whether on the scaffold high
"Or the battle-field we die,
"Oh, what matter, when for Erin dear we fall!"

IV.

Never till the latest day
Shall the memory pass away
Of the gallant lives thus given for our land;
But on the cause must go,
Amidst joy, or weal, or woe,
Till we've made our isle a nation free and grand.
"God save Ireland!" say we proudly;
"God save Ireland!" say we all:
"Whether on the scaffold high
"Or the battle-field we die,
"Oh, what matter, when for Erin dear we fall!"

28

Resolutions of the Home Rule Conference, 1873

In 1870 Isaac Butt began the Home Rule movement, forming the Home Government Association. At a conference in 1873, this was transformed into a full-fledged political party, the Home Rule League, with a moderate federalist program.

Source: Curtis and McDowell, 276–78 (see document 4); from *Proceedings of the home rule conference held in the Rotunda, Dublin, the 18, 19, 20, and 21 November 1873* (Dublin, 1873), 201–2.

1. That as the basis of the proceedings of this conference, we declare our conviction that it is essentially necessary to the peace and prosperity of Ireland that the right of domestic legislation on all Irish affairs should be restored to our country.

2. That, solemnly reasserting the inalienable right of the Irish people to self-government, we declare that the time in our opinion has come when a combined and energetic effort should be made to obtain the restoration of that right.

3. That, in accordance with the ancient and constitutional rights of the Irish nation, we claim the privilege of managing our own affairs by a parliament assembled in Ireland, and composed of the sovereign, the lords, and the commons of Ireland.

4. That, in claiming these rights and privileges for our country, we adopt the principle of a federal arrangement, which would secure to the Irish parliament the right of legislating for and regulating all matters relating to the internal affairs of Ireland, while leaving to the imperial parliament the power of dealing with all questions affecting the imperial crown and government, legislation regarding the colonies and other dependencies of the crown, the relations of the empire with foreign states, and all matters appertaining to the defence and stability of the empire at large, as well as the power of granting the supplies necessary for imperial purposes.

5. That, such an arrangement does not involve any change in the existing constitution of the imperial parliament, or any interference with the prerogatives of the crown or disturbance of the principles of the constitution.

6. That to secure to the Irish people the advantages of constitutional government, it is essential that there should be in Ireland an administration for Irish affairs, controlled, according to constitutional principles, by the Irish parliament, and conducted by ministers constitutionally responsible to that parliament.

7. That in the opinion of this conference, a federal arrangement, based upon these principles, would consolidate the strength and maintain the integrity of the empire, and add to the dignity and power of the imperial crown.

8. That while we believe that in an Irish parliament the rights and liberties of all classes of our countrymen would find their best and surest protection, we are willing that there should be incorporated in the federal constitution articles supplying the amplest guarantees that no change shall be made by that parliament in the present settlement of property in Ireland, and that no legislation shall be adopted to establish any religious ascen-

dancy in Ireland, or to subject any person to disabilities on account of his religious opinions.

9. That this conference cannot separate without calling on the Irish constituencies at the next general election, to return men earnestly and truly devoted to the great cause which this conference has been called to promote, and who in any emergency that may arise may be ready to take counsel with a great national conference, to be called in such a manner as to represent the opinions and feelings of the Irish nation; and that, with a view of rendering members of parliament and their constituents more in accord on all questions affecting the welfare of the country, it is recommended by this conference that at the close of each session of parliament the representatives should render to their constituents an account of their stewardships.

10. That in order to carry these objects into practical effect, an association be now formed to be called 'The Irish Home Rule league' of which the essential and fundamental principles shall be those declared in the resolutions adopted at this conference, and of which the object, and the only object, shall be to obtain for Ireland by peaceable and constitutional means, the self-government claimed in those resolutions.

29

Charles Stewart Parnell on the Land Question, 1880

By 1880 Parnell had emerged as the leader of the Home Rule movement and joined it to the agitation for land reform. This speech at Ennis, September 19, 1880, at the height of the "Land War," is an example of his popular oratory, in the tradition of O'Connell, his predecessor as charismatic national leader. His suggestion of "a moral Coventry" (an English term for shunning) relates to the practice known as "boycotting" after its first victim.

Source: *The Freeman's Journal*, September 20, 1880, 7.

Depend upon it that the measure of the land bill of next session will be the measure of your activity and energy this winter *(cheers)*—it will be the measure of your determination not to pay unjust rents—it will be the measure of your determination to keep a firm grip of your homesteads *(cheers)*. It will be the measure of your determination not to bid for farms from which others have been evicted, and to use the strong force of pubic opinion to deter any unjust men amongst yourselves—and there are many such—from bidding for such farms (*hear, hear*). If you refuse to pay unjust rents, if you refuse to take farms from which others have been evicted, the land question must be settled, and settled in a way that will be satisfactory to you. . . . Now, what are you to do to a tenant who bids for a farm from which another tenant has been evicted?

(Several voices). Shoot him.

(Mr. Parnell). I think I heard somebody say shoot him *(cheers).* I wish to point out to you a very much better way—a more christian and charitable way, which will give the lost man an opportunity of repenting *(laughter, and hear).* When a man takes a farm from which another has been evicted you must shun him on the roadside when you meet him—you must shun him in the streets of the town—you must shun him in the shop—you must shun him in the fair-green and in the market place, and even in the place of worship, by leaving him alone, by putting him into a moral Coventry, by isolating him from the rest of his country as if he were the leper of old—you must show him your detestation of the crime he has committed. If you do this, you may depend on it there will be no man so full of avarice—so lost to shame—as to dare the public opinion of all the right-thinking men in the county and transgress your unwritten code of laws. . . . The feudal system of land tenure has been tried in almost every European country and it has been found wanting everywhere; but nowhere has it brought more exile, produced more suffering, crime and destitution than in Ireland *(cheers).* It was abolished in Prussia by transferring the land from the landlords to the occupying tenants. The landlords were given government paper as compensation. Let the English government give the landlords their paper to-morrow as compensation *(laughter).* We want no money—not a single penny of money would be necessary. Why, if they gave the Irish landlords—the bad section of them—the four or five millions a year that they spend on the police and military *(groans)* in helping them to collect their rents, that would be a solution of it *(cheers),* and a very

cheap solution of it. . . . In my opinion the longer the landlords wait, the worse the settlement they will get *(cheers)*. Now is the time for them to settle before the people learn the power of combination. We have been accused of preaching communistic doctrines when we told the people not to pay an unjust rent, and the flowing out of that advice in a few of the Irish counties had shown the English government the necessity for a radical alteration in the land laws. But how would they like it if we told the people some day or other not to pay any rent until this question is settled *(cheers)*. . . . It will be for the consideration of wiser heads than mine whether, if the landlords continue obdurate, and refuse all just concessions, we shall not be obliged to tell the people of Ireland to strike against rent until this question has been settled *(cheers)*. And if the five hundred thousand tenant farmers of Ireland struck against the ten thousand landlords, I would like to see where they would get police and soldiers enough to make them pay *(loud cheers)*.

30

Irish Parliamentary Party Pledge, 1885

Parnell succeed in imposing a tight discipline on the Home Rule party in Parliament, as illustrated by this pledge signed by the candidates at the Wicklow convention in 1885.
Source: *Freeman's Journal*, October 6, 1885, 5.

I pledge myself that in the event of my election to Parliament I will sit, act, and vote with the Irish Parliamentary Party; and if at a meeting of the party, convened upon due notice specially to consider the question, it be determined by a resolution, supported by a majority of the entire Parliamentary Party that I have not fulfilled the above pledge, I hereby undertake forthwith to resign my seat.

31

William Ewart Gladstone: First Home Rule Bill Speech (1886)

William Ewart Gladstone, four times Liberal Prime Minister, was converted to Home Rule just before his third term (1886) and introduced what was to be the first of three Home Rule Bills. These excerpts from a nearly four-hour speech introducing the bill (April 8, 1886) show both his recognition of Irish nationality and his plan to reconcile Irish autonomy with the continuance of the United Kingdom. The bill failed, but the commitment to Home Rule did not.

Source: *The Past Speaks since 1688*, ed. Walter L. Arnstein (Lexington, MA: D.C. Heath & Co., 1981), 268–72, copyright © by Houghton Mifflin Company; from *Hansard's Parliamentary Debates*, 3rd ser., vol. CCCIV, cols. 1038–85.

. . . In point of fact, law is discredited in Ireland, and discredited in Ireland upon this ground especially—that it comes to the people of that country with a foreign aspect, and in a foreign garb. These Coercion Bills of ours, of course—for it has become a matter of course—I am speaking of the facts and not of the merits—these Coercion Bills are stiffly resisted by the Members who represent Ireland in Parliament. The English mind, by cases of this kind and by the tone of the Press towards them, is estranged from the Irish people and the Irish mind is estranged from the people of England and Scotland. . . .

The case of Ireland, though she is represented here not less fully than England or Scotland, is not the same as that of England or Scotland. . . .

The mainspring of law in England is felt by the people to be English; the mainspring of law in Scotland is felt by the people to be Scotch; but the mainspring of law in Ireland is not felt by the people to be Irish. . . . It is a problem not unknown in the history of the world; it is really this—there can be no secret about it as far as we are concerned—how to reconcile Imperial unity with diversity of legislation. Mr. Grattan not only held these purposes to be reconcilable, but he did not scruple to go the length of saying this—

> I demand the continued severance of the Parliaments with a view to the continued and everlasting unity of the Empire.

. . . I cannot conceal the conviction that the voice of Ireland, as a whole, is at this moment clearly and Constitutionally spoken. I cannot say it is otherwise when five-sixths of its lawfully chosen Representatives are of one mind in this matter. There is a counter voice; and I wish to know what is the claim of those by whom that counter voice is spoken, and how much is the scope and allowance we can give them. Certainly, Sir, I cannot allow it to be said that a Protestant minority in Ulster, or elsewhere, is to rule the question at large for Ireland. . . .

The capital article of that Legislative Body will be that it should have the control of the Executive Government of Ireland as well as of legislative Business. . . .

I will now tell the House—and I would beg particular attention to this—what are the functions that we propose to withdraw from the cognizance of this Legislative Body. The three grand and principal functions are, first, everything that relates to the Crown. . . . The next would be all that belongs to defence—the Army, the Navy, the entire organization of armed force. . . . And the third would be the entire subject of Foreign and Colonial relations. . . . We propose to provide that the Legislative Body should not be competent to pass a law for the establishment or the endowment of any particular religion. Those I may call exceptions of principle. . . .

. . . . It is commonly said in England and Scotland—and in the main it is, I think, truly said—that we have for a great number of years been struggling to pass good laws for Ireland. We have sacrificed our time; we have neglected our own business; we have advanced our money—which I do not think at all a great favour conferred on her—and all this in the endeavour to give Ireland good laws. . . . Sir, I do not deny the general good intentions of Parliament on a variety of great and conspicuous occasions, and its desire to pass good laws for Ireland. But let me say that, in order to work out the purposes of government, there is something more in this world occasionally required than even the passing of good laws. It is sometimes requisite not only that good laws should be passed, but also that they should be passed by the proper persons. . . .

We stand face to face with what is termed Irish nationality. . . .

I ask that in our own case we should practice with firm and fearless hand, what we have so often preached . . . namely, that the concession of local self-government is not the way to sap or impair, but the way to strengthen and consolidate unity . . . and it is thus, by the decree of the Almighty, that we may be enabled to secure at once the social peace, the fame, the power, and the permanence of Empire.

32

Douglas Hyde:
"The Necessity for
De-Anglicising Ireland"
(1892)

Douglas Hyde, himself a Protestant and apolitical as regards nationalism, was a pioneer of the cultural Gaelic Revival, cofounding the Gaelic League in 1893. This lecture to the National Literary Society, Dublin, November 25, 1892, may be considered the manifesto of the "Irish-Ireland" movement. The frequent references to "race," which seem objectionable nowadays, were commonplace of the time, usually directed against the Irish; Hyde at least reclaimed "the Irish race" for Irishmen. He was later to be named the first President of Eire as a symbol of national unity.

Source: Reprinted by permission from Arthur Mitchell and Pádraig Ó Snodaigh (eds.), *Irish Political Documents 1869-1916*, 81-86, published by Irish Academic Press, 44 Northumberland Road, Ballsbridge, Dublin 4, Ireland. Copyright Irish Academic Press (1989).

. . . .If we take a bird's-eye view of our island to-day, and compare it with what it used to be, we must be struck by the extraordinary fact that the nation which once was, as every one admits, one of the most classically learned and cultured nations in Europe, is now one of the least so; how one of the most reading and literary peoples has become one of the *least* studious and most *un*-literary, and how the present art products of one of the quickest, most sensitive, and most artistic races on earth are now only distinguished for their hideousness.

I shall endeavour to show that this failure of the Irish people in recent times has been largely brought about by the race diverging during this century from the right path, and ceasing to be Irish without becoming English. I shall attempt to show that with the bulk of the people this change took place quite recently, much more recently than most people imagine, and is, in fact, still going on. I should also like to call attention to the illogical position of men who drop their own language to speak English, of men who translate their euphonious Irish names into English monosyllables, of men who read English books, and know nothing about Gaelic literature, nevertheless protesting as a matter of sentiment that they hate the country which at every hand's turn they rush to imitate.

. . . . It has always been very curious to me how Irish sentiment sticks in this half-way house—how it continues to apparently hate the English, and at the same time continues to imitate them; how it continues to clamour for recognition as a distinction nationality, and at the same time throws away with both hands what would make it so. . . . It is just because there appears no earthly chance of their becoming good members of the Empire that I urge that they become the other; cultivate what they have rejected, and build up an Irish nation on Irish lines.

But you ask, why should we wish to make Ireland more Celtic than it is—why should we de-Anglicise it at all?

I answer because the Irish race is at present in a most anomalous position, imitating England and yet apparently hating it.

How can it produce anything good in literature, art, or institutions as long as it is actuated by motives so contradictory? Besides, I believe it is our Gaelic past which, though the Irish race does not recognise it just at present, is really at the bottom of the Irish heart. . . .

We have at last broken the continuity of Irish life, and just at the moment when the Celtic race is presumably about to largely recover possession of its own country, it finds itself deprived and stript of its Celtic characteristics, cut off from the past, yet scarcely in touch with the present. It has lost since the beginning of this century almost all that connected it with the era of Cuchullain and of Ossian, that connected it with the Christianisers of Europe, that connected it with Brian Boru and the heroes of Clontarf, with the O'Neills and O'Donnells, with Rory O'More, with the Wild Geese, and even to some extent with the men of '98. It has lost all that they had—language, traditions, music, genius, and ideas. Just when we should be starting to build up anew the Irish race and the Gaelic nation-as within our own recollection Greece has been built up anew— we find ourselves despoiled of the bricks of nationality. . . .

The bulk of the Irish race really lived in the closest contact with the tradition of the past and the national life of nearly eighteen hundred years, until the beginning of this century. Not only so, but during the whole of the dark Penal times they produced amongst themselves a most vigorous literary development. . . . This training, however, nearly every one of fair education during the Penal times possessed, nor did they begin to lose their Irish training and knowledge until after the establishment of Maynooth and the rise of O'Connell. These two events made an end of the Gaelicism of the Gaelic race, although a great number of poets and scribes existed even down to the forties and fifties of the present century, and a few may linger on yet in remote localities. But it may be said, roughly speaking, that the ancient Gaelic civilisation died with O'Connell, largely, I am afraid, owing to his example and his neglect of inculcating the necessity of keeping alive racial customs, language, and traditions, in which with the one notable exception of our scholarly idealist, Smith O'Brien, he has been followed until a year ago by almost every leader of the Irish race.

Thomas Davis and his brilliant band of Young Irelanders came just at the dividing of the line, and tried to give to Ireland a new literature in English to replace the literature which was just being discarded. It succeeded and it did not succeed. It was a most brilliant effort, but the old bark had been too recently stripped off the Irish tree, and the trunk could not take as it might have done to a fresh one. . . .

In conclusion, I would earnestly appeal to every one, whether Unionist or Nationalist, who wishes to see the Irish nation produce its best—and surely whatever our politics are we all wish that—to set his face against this constant running to England for our books, literature, music, games, fashions, and ideas. I appeal to every one whatever his politics—for this is no political matter—to do his best to help the Irish race to develop in future upon Irish lines, even at the risk of encouraging national aspirations, because upon Irish lines alone can the Irish race once more become what it was of yore—one of the most original, artistic, literary, and charming people of Europe.

33

Solemn League and Covenant, 1912

Practically all Protestant Ulstermen signed this pledge to resist the imposition of Home Rule, virtually assured of enactment. The title is drawn from a seventeenth-century document of Presbyterian solidarity.

Source: Reprinted by permission from Arthur Mitchell and Pádraig Ó Snodaigh (eds.), *Irish Political Documents 1869-1916*, 136, published by Irish Academic Press, 44 Northumberland Road, Ballsbridge, Dublin 4, Ireland. Copyright Irish Academic Press (1989).

Being convinced in our consciences that Home Rule would be disastrous to the material well-being of Ulster as well as the whole of Ireland, subversive of our civil and religious freedom, destructive of our citizenship and perilous to the unity of the Empire, we, whose names are underwritten, men of Ulster, loyal subjects of His Gracious Majesty King George V, humbly relying on the God whom our fathers in days of stress and trial confidently trusted, do hereby pledge ourselves in solemn Covenant throughout this our time of threatened calamity to stand by one another in defending for ourselves and our children our cherished position of equal citizenship in the United Kingdom and in using all means which may be found necessary to defeat the present conspiracy to set up a Home Rule Parliament in Ireland. And in the event of such a Parliament being forced upon us we further solemnly and mutually pledge ourselves to refuse to recognise its authority. In sure confidence that God will defend the right we hereto subscribe our names. And further, we individually declare that we have not already signed this Covenant.

The above was signed by me at _____

'Ulster Day,' Saturday, 28th September, 1912.

God Save the King.

34

Proclamation of the Irish Republic, 1916

This proclamation, read by Patrick Pearse at the Post Office in Dublin on April 24, 1916, signaled the beginning of the Easter rising. All the signatories were among those shot by the British military.
Source: O'Day and Stevenson, 160–61.

Poblacht na h-Éireann

The Provisional Government of the Irish Republic to the People of Ireland

Irishmen and Irishwomen: In the name of God and of the dead generations from which she receives her old tradition of nationhood, Ireland, through us, summons her children to her flag and strikes for her freedom.

Having organised and trained her manhood through her secret revolutionary organisation, the Irish Republican Brotherhood, and through her open military organisations, the Irish Volunteers, and the Irish Citizen Army, having patiently perfected her discipline, having resolutely waited for the right moment to reveal itself, she now seizes that moment, and, supported by her exiled children in America and by gallant allies in Europe, but relying in the first on her own strength, she strikes in full confidence of victory.

We declare the right of the people of Ireland to the ownership of Ireland, and to the unfettered control of Irish destinies, to be sovereign and indefeasible. The long usurpation of that right by a foreign people and government has not extinguished the right, nor can it ever be extinguished except by the destruction of the Irish people. In every generation the Irish people have asserted their right to national freedom and sovereignty; six times during the past three hundred years they have asserted it in arms. Standing on that fundamental right and again asserting it in arms in the face of the world, we hereby proclaim the Irish Republic as a sovereign independent state, and we pledge our lives and the lives of our comrades-in-arms to the cause of its freedom, of its welfare, and of its exaltation among the nations.

The Irish Republic is entitled to, and hereby claims, the allegiance of every Irishman and Irishwoman. The Republic guarantees religious and civil liberty, equal rights and equal opportunities to all its citizens, and declares its resolve to pursue the happiness and prosperity of the whole nation and of all its parts, cherishing all the children of the nation equally, and oblivious of the differences carefully fostered by an alien government, which have divided a minority from the majority in the past.

Until our arms have brought the opportune moment for the establishment of a permanent national government, representative of the whole people of Ireland, and elected by the suffrages of all her men and women, the Provisional Government, hereby constituted, will administer the civil and military affairs of the Republic in trust for the people. We place the cause of the Irish

Republic under the protection of the Most High God, whose blessing we invoke upon our arms, and we pray that no one who serves the cause will dishonour it by cowardice, inhumanity, or rapine. In this supreme hour the Irish Nation must, by its valour and discipline, and by the readiness of its children to sacrifice themselves for the common good, prove itself worthy of the august destiny to which it is called.

Signed on behalf of the provisional government,

Thomas J. Clarke, Sean Mac Diarmada, Thomas MacDonagh, P. H. Pearse, Eamonn Ceannt, James Connolly, Joseph Plunkett

35

Government of Ireland Act, 1920

Ireland was in a state of civil war in 1920, when the Home Rule Act passed in 1912–14 should have gone into effect but had been superseded by events. Prime Minister David Lloyd George, a Liberal leading a largely Conservative coalition, produced this act providing for *two* Home Rules, one for Northern Ireland (the six Protestant-dominated counties of Ulster) and one for Southern Ireland (the rest). Southern Ireland rejected this Home Rule, continuing the civil war until it obtained dominion status under the Treaty of 1921. Northern Ireland accepted its Home Rule and formed a government under its terms, which remained in being after the treaty. The provisions for each of the Home Rule entities are substantially the same as those proposed for all Ireland in the earlier Home Rule bills, showing what Home Rule meant in law. This is the act under which Northern Ireland was actually governed from 1921 to 1972—although Northern Ireland did not live up to the nondiscrimination provisions of section 5. The omitted sections 2 and 3 refer to a proposed Council of Ireland and the possibility of the two Parliaments merging; they never went into effect.

Source: Reprinted by permission from Arthur Mitchell and Pádraig Ó Snodaigh (eds.), *Irish Political Documents 1916–1949*, 91–96, published by Irish Academic Press, 44 Northumberland Road, Ballsbridge, Dublin 4, Ireland. Copyright Irish Academic Press (1985). From *Acts parl. U.K., 1920:* 10 & 11 Geo. V, c. 67.

An Act to Provide For The Better Government
Of Ireland. 23rd December 1920.

Be it enacted by the King's most Excellent Majesty, by and with
the advice and consent of the Lords Spiritual and Temporal, and
Commons, in this present Parliament assembled, and by the
authority of the same, as follows: ESTABLISHMENT OF PAR-
LIAMENTS FOR SOUTHERN IRELAND AND NORTHERN
IRELAND AND A COUNCIL OF IRELAND.

1. – (1) On and after the appointed day there shall be established for Southern Ireland a Parliament to be called the Parliament of Southern Ireland consisting of His Majesty, the Senate
of Southern Ireland, and the House of Commons of Southern
Ireland, and there shall be established for Northern Ireland a
Parliament to be called the Parliament of Northern Ireland consisting of His Majesty, the Senate of Northern Ireland, and the
House of Commons of Northern Ireland.

(2) For the purposes of this Act, Northern Ireland shall
consist of the parliamentary counties of Antrim, Armagh, Down,
Fermanagh, Londonderry and Tyrone, and the parliamentary
boroughs of Belfast and Londonderry, and Southern Ireland shall
consist of so much of Ireland as is not comprised within the said
parliamentary counties and boroughs. . . .

4. – (1) Subject to the provisions of this Act, the Parliament of Southern Ireland and the Parliament of Northern Ireland shall respectively have power to make laws for the peace,
order, and good government of Southern Ireland and Northern Ireland with the following limitations, namely, that they
shall not have power to make laws except in respect of matters exclusively relating to the portion of Ireland within their
jurisdiction, or some part thereof, and (without prejudice to
that general limitation) that they shall not have power to make

114

laws in respect of the following matters in particular, namely:—

(1) The Crown or the succession to the Crown, or a regency, or the property of the Crown (including foreshore vested in the Crown), or the Lord Lieutenant, except as respects the exercise of his executive power in relation to Irish services as defined for the purposes of this Act; or

(2) The making of peace or war, or matters arising from a state of war; or the regulation of the conduct of any portion of His Majesty's subjects during the existence of hostilities between foreign states with which His Majesty is at peace, in relation to those hostilities; or

(3) The navy, the army, the air force, the territorial force, or any other naval, military, or air force, or the defence of the realm, or any other naval, military, or air force matter (including any pensions and allowances payable to persons who have been members of or in respect of service in any such force or their widows or dependants, and provision for the training, education, employment and assistance for the reinstatement in civil life of persons who have ceased to be members of any such force); or

(4) Treaties, or any relations with foreign states, or relations with other parts of His Majesty's dominions, or matters involving the contravention of treaties or agreements with foreign states or any part of His Majesty's dominions, or offences connected with any such treaties or relations, or procedure connected with the extradition of criminals under any treaty, or the return of fugitive offenders from or to any part of His Majesty's dominions; or

(5) Dignities or titles of honour; or

(6) Treason, treason felony, alienage, naturalization, or aliens as such, or domicile; or

(7) Trade with any place out of the part of Ireland within

115

their jurisdiction, except so far as trade may be affected by the exercise of the powers of taxation given to the said parliaments, or by regulations made for the sole purpose of preventing contagious disease, or by steps taken by means of inquiries or agencies out of the part of Ireland within their jurisdiction for the improvement of the trade of that part or for the protection of trades of that part from fraud; the granting of bounties on the export of goods; quarantine; navigation, including merchant shipping (except as respects inland waters, the regulation of harbours, and local health regulations); or

(8) Submarine cables; or

(9) Wireless telegraphy; or

(10) Aerial navigation; or

(11) Lighthouses, buoys, or beacons (except so far as they can consistently with any general Act of Parliament of the United Kingdom be constructed or maintained by a local harbour authority); or

(12) Coinage; legal tender; negotiable instruments (including bank notes) except so far as negotiable instruments may be affected by the exercise of the powers of taxation given to the said Parliaments; or any change in the standard of weights and measures; or

(13) Trade marks, designs, merchandise marks, copyright, or patent rights; or

(14) Any matter which by this Act is declared to be a reserved matter, so long as it remains reserved. Any law made in contravention of the limitations imposed by this section shall, so far as it contravenes those limitations, be void. . . .

5. – (1) In the exercise of their power to make laws under this Act neither the Parliament of Southern Ireland nor the Parliament of Northern Ireland shall make a law so as either directly or indirectly to establish or endow any religion, or prohibit

or restrict the free exercise thereof, or give a preference, privilege, or advantage, or impose any disability or disadvantage, on account of religious belief or religious or ecclesiastical status, or make any religious belief or religious ceremony a condition of the validity of any marriage, or affect prejudicially the right of any child to attend a school receiving public money without attending the religious instruction at the school, or alter the constitution of any religious body except where the alteration is approved on behalf of the religious body by the governing body thereof, or divert from any religious denomination the fabric of cathedral churches, or, except for the purpose of roads, railways, lighting, water, or drainage works, or other works of public utility upon payment of compensation, any other property, or take any property without compensation. Any law made in contravention of the restrictions imposed by this subsection shall, so far as it contravenes those restrictions, be void.

(2) Any existing enactment by which any penalty, disadvantage, or disability is imposed on account of religious belief or on a member of any religious order as such shall, as from the appointed day, cease to have effect in Ireland.

36

Irish Free State Agreement Act (1922)

This enactment by the British Parliament was necessary to give the force of law to the "Treaty" negotiated in December 1921 and ratified by the majority of the Dáil in 1922. Northern Ireland opted out under article 12. *Source: Public General Statutes*, LX, 4–12; 23 Geo. V, c. 4.

An act to give the force of Law to certain Articles of Agreement for a Treaty between Great Britain and Ireland and to enable effect to be given thereto, and for other purposes incidental thereto and consequential thereon. Be it enacted . . . as follows:—

1. The Articles of Agreement for a treaty between Great Britain and Ireland set forth in the Schedule to this Act shall have the force of law as from the date of the passing of this Act . . . .

ARTICLES OF AGREEMENT. . . .

1. Ireland shall have the same constitutional status, in the Community of Nations known as the British Empire as the Dominion of Canada, the Commonwealth of Australia, the Dominion of New Zealand, and the Union of South Africa, with a Parliament having powers to make laws for the peace

order and good government of Ireland, and an Executive responsible to that Parliament, and shall be styled and known as the Irish Free State.

2. Subject to the provisions hereinafter set out, the position of the Irish Free State in relation to the Imperial Parliament and Government and otherwise shall be that of the Dominion of Canada, and the law, practice, and constitutional usage governing the relationship of the Crown or the representative of the Crown and of the Imperial Parliament to the Dominion of Canada shall govern their relationship to the Irish Free State.

3. The representative of the Crown in Ireland shall be appointed in like manner as the Governor-General of Canada and in accordance with the practice observed in the making of such appointments.

❈ 4. The oath to be taken by Members of the Parliament of the Irish Free State shall be in the following form:—

"I, ... , do solemnly swear true faith and allegiance to the Constitution of the Irish Free State as by law established, and that I will be faithful to H.M. King George V, his heirs and successors by law in virtue of the common citizenship of Ireland with Great Britain and her adherence to and membership of the group of nations forming the British Commonwealth of Nations." . . .

11. Until the expiration of one month from the passing of the Act of Parliament for the ratification of this instrument, the powers of the Parliament and the Government of the Irish Free State shall not be exercisable as respects Northern Ireland. . . .

12. If, before the expiration of the said month, an address is presented to His Majesty by both Houses of the Parliament of Northern Ireland to that effect, the powers of the parliament and government of the Irish Free State shall no longer extend to Northern Ireland. . . .

16. Neither the Parliament of the Irish Free State nor the Parliament of Northern Ireland shall make any law so as either directly or indirectly to endow any religion or prohibit or restrict the free exercise thereof or give any preference or impose any disability on account of religious belief or religious status or affect prejudicially the right of any child to attend a school receiving public money without attending the religious instruction at the school, or make any discrimination as respects State aid between schools under the management of different religious denominations or divert from any religious denomination or any educational institution any of its property except for public utility purposes and on payment of compensation.

17. By way of provisional arrangement for the administration of Southern Ireland during the interval which must elapse between the date hereof and the constitution of a Parliament and Government of the Irish Free State in accordance therewith, steps shall be taken forthwith for summoning a meeting of members of Parliament elected for constituencies in Southern Ireland since the passing of the Government of Ireland Act, 1920, and for constituting a provisional Government, and the British Government shall take the steps necessary to transfer to such provisional Government the powers and machinery requisite for the discharge of its duties, provided that every member of such provisional Government shall have signified in writing his or her acceptance of this instrument. But this arrangement shall not continue in force beyond the expiration of twelve months from the date hereof. . . .

37

Constitution of the Irish Free State (1922)

This democratic constitution was adopted by the newly elected Dáil in the midst of the civil war which accompanied the founding of the Free State. It incorporates the controversial oath specified in the Treaty.

Source: Saorstát Éireann, *The Constitution of the Irish Free State (Saorstát Éireann) Act, 1922, and the Public General Acts,* 5–43.

Constitution of the Irish Free State (Saorstát Éireann)

Article 1.

The Irish Free State (otherwise hereinafter called or sometimes called Saorstát Éireann) is a co-equal member of the Community of Nations forming the British Commonwealth of Nations.

Article 2.

All powers of government and all authority, legislative, executive, and judicial in Ireland, are derived from the people of Ireland and the same shall be exercised in the Irish Free State

(Saorstát Éireann) through the organisations established by or under, and in accord with, this Constitution.

Article 3.

Every person, without distinction of sex, domiciled in the area of the jurisdiction of the Irish Free State (Saorstát Éireann) at the time of the coming into operation of this Constitution who was born in Ireland or either of whose parents was born in Ireland or who has been ordinarily resident in the area of the jurisdiction of the Irish Free State (Saorstát Éireann) for not less than seven years, is a citizen of the Irish Free State (Saorstát Éireann) and shall within the limits of the jurisdiction of the Irish Free State (Saorstát Éireann) enjoy the privileges and be subject to the obligations of such citizenship: Provided that any such person being a citizen of another State may elect not to accept the citizenship hereby conferred; and the conditions governing the future acquisition and termination of citizenship in the Irish Free State (Saorstát Éireann) shall be determined by law.

Article 4.

The National language of the Irish Free State (Saorstát Éireann) is the Irish language, but the English language shall be equally recognised as an official language. Nothing in this Article shall prevent special provisions being made by the Parliament of the Irish Free State (otherwise called and herein generally referred to as the 'Oireachtas') for districts or areas in which only one language is in general use. . . .

Article 6.

The liberty of the person is inviolable, and no person shall be deprived of his liberty except in accordance with law. Upon complaint made by or on behalf of any person that he is being unlawfully detained, the High Court and any and every judge thereof shall forthwith enquire into the same and may make an order requiring the person in whose custody such person shall be detained to produce the body of the person so detained before such Court or judge without delay and to certify in writing as to the cause of the detention and such Court or judge shall thereupon order the release of such person unless satisfied that he is being detained in accordance with the law:

Provided, however, that nothing in this Article contained shall be invoked to prohibit control or interfere with any act of the military forces of the Irish Free State (Saorstát Éireann) during the existence of a state of war or armed rebellion. . . .

Article 8.

Freedom of conscience and the free profession and practice of religion are, subject to public order and morality, guaranteed to every citizen, and no law may be made either directly or indirectly to endow any religion, or prohibit or restrict the free exercise thereof or give any preference, or impose any disability on account of religious belief or religious status, or affect prejudicially the right of any child to attend a school receiving public money without attending the religious instruction at the school, or make any discrimination as respects State aid between schools under the management of different religious denominations, or divert from any religious denomination or any educational institution any of its property except for the purpose of roads, railways, lighting, water or drainage works or other works of public utility, and on payment of compensation.

Article 9.

The right of free expression of opinion as well as the right to assemble peacefully and without arms, and to form associations or unions is guaranteed for purposes not opposed to public morality. Law regulating the manner in which the right of forming associations and the right of free assembly may be exercised shall contain no political, religious or class distinction.

Article 10.

All citizens of the Irish Free State (Saorstát Éireann) have the right to free elementary education. . . .

Article 12.

A Legislature is hereby created to be known as the Oireachtas. It shall consist of the King and two Houses, the Chamber of Deputies (otherwise called and herein generally referred to as "Dáil Éireann") and the Senate (otherwise called and herein generally referred to as "Seanad Éireann"). The sole and exclusive power of making laws for the peace, order and good government of the Irish Free State (Saorstát Éireann) is vested in the Oireachtas. . . .

Article 14.

All citizens of the Irish Free State (Saorstát Éireann) without distinction of sex, who have reached the age of twenty-one years and who comply with the provisions of the prevailing electoral laws, shall have the right to vote for members of Dáil Éireann, and to take part in the Referendum and Initiative. All citizens of the Irish Free State (Saorstát Éireann) without distinction of sex who have reached the age of thirty years and who comply with the provisions of the prevailing electoral laws, shall have the right to vote for members of Seanad Éireann. . . .

124

Article 17.

The oath to be taken by members of the Oireachtas shall be in the following form:

> I . . . do solemnly swear true faith and allegiance to the Constitution of the Irish Free State as by law established, and that I will be faithful to H.M. King George V., his heirs and successors by law in virtue of the common citizenship of Ireland with Great Britain and her adherence to and membership of the group of nations forming the British Commonwealth of Nations.
> Such oath shall be taken and subscribed by every member of the Oireachtas before taking his seat therein before the Representative of the Crown or some person authorised by him.

38

Constitution of Éire (1937)

The ideological flavoring of this constitution, the work of Eamon DeValera, contrasts with the relative neutrality of the 1922 constitution. All references to the British connection are eliminated (but not abolished).

Source: O'Day and Stevenson, 194–96; from *Bunreacht na hÉirann* (Dublin Stationery Office, 1937), 2–8, 138–44.

In the Name of the Most Holy Trinity, from Whom is all authority and to Whom, as our final end, all actions both of men and States must be referred,

We, the people of Éire,

Humbly acknowledging all our obligations to our Divine Lord, Jesus Christ, Who sustained our fathers through centuries of trial,

Gratefully remembering their heroic and unremitting struggle to regain the rightful independence of our Nation,

And seeking to promote the common good, with due observance of Prudence, Justice and Charity, so that the dignity and freedom of the individual may be assured, true social order attained, the unity of our country restored, and concord established with other nations,

Do hereby adopt, enact, and give to ourselves this Constitution.

The Nation

Article 1.

The Irish nation hereby affirms its inalienable, indefeasible, and sovereign right to choose its own form of Government, to determine its relations with other nations, and to develop its life, political, economic and cultural, in accordance with its own genius and traditions.

Article 2.

The national territory consists of the whole island of Ireland, its islands and territorial seas.

Article 3.

Pending the re-integration of the national territory, and without prejudice to the right of the Parliament and Government established by this Constitution to exercise jurisdiction over the whole of that territory, the laws enacted by that parliament shall have the like area and extent of application as the laws Saorstát Éireann and the like extra-territorial effect.

The State

Article 4.

The name of the State is Éire, or in the English language, Ireland.

Article 5.

Ireland is a sovereign, independent, democratic state.

Article 6.

1. All powers of government, legislative, executive and judicial, derive, under God, from the people, whose right it is to

designate the rulers of the State and, in final appeal, to decide all questions of national policy, according to the requirements of the common good.

2. These powers of government are exercisable only by or on the authority of the organs of State established by this Constitution.

Article 7.

The national flag is the tricolour of green, white and orange.

Article 8.

1. The Irish language as the national language is the first official language.

2. The English language is recognised as a second official language.

3. Provision may, however, be made by law for the exclusive use of either of the said languages for any one or more official purposes, either throughout the State or in any part thereof.

Article 9.

.... 2. Fidelity to the nation and loyalty to the State are fundamental political duties of all citizens. ....

Article 41.

3. 1° The State pledges itself to guard with special care the institution of Marriage, on which the Family is founded, and to protect it against attack.

2° No law shall be enacted providing for the grant of a dissolution of marriage.

3° No person whose marriage has been dissolved under the civil law of any other State but is a subsisting valid marriage under the law for the time being in force within the jurisdiction of the Government and Parliament established by this Constitution shall be capable of contracting a valid marriage within the jurisdiction during the lifetime of the other party to the marriage so dissolved. . . .

Article 44.

1° The State acknowledges that the homage of public worship is due to Almighty God. It shall hold His Name in reverence, and shall respect and honour religion.

2° The State recognises the special position of the Holy Catholic Apostolic and Roman Church as the guardian of the Faith professed by the great majority of its citizens.

3° The State also recognises the Church of Ireland, the Presbyterian Church in Ireland, the Methodist Church in Ireland, the Religious Society of Friends in Ireland, as well as the Jewish Congregations and the other religious denominations existing in Ireland at the date of the coming into operation of this Constitution.

39

Eamon De Valera:
Reply to Churchill on
the Ports (1940)

Eamon de Valera, now Taoiseach of Éire, was committed to a policy of
neutrality in any European war, as a sign of Ireland's independence. In
1938 he had obtained the retrocession of the naval bases which Britain had
kept under the Treaty of 1921. These would have been useful in dealing
with the German submarine menace in World War II, and the British Prime
Minister Winston Churchill made repeated demands to be given the use of
the ports. One such remark produced this reply in the Dáil on November 6,
1940. It shows De Valera's determination to stay neutral; it also shows his
political skill in creating a crisis in which he would prevail. Ireland remained neutral.

Source: Reprinted by permission from Arthur Mitchell and Pádraig Ó
Snodaigh (eds.), *Irish Political Documents 1916-1949,* 222-24, published
by Irish Academic Press, 44 Northumberland Road, Ballsbridge, Dublin
4, Ireland. Copyright Irish Academic Press (1985). From *Dáil Éireann
Debates*, vol. 81, 582–86, 6 November 1940.

. . . I think that every Deputy, when he read the statement of
the British Prime Minister with reference to our ports, must have

130

wondered somewhat. . . . I would have refrained from making any comment upon it were it not that it has been followed by an extensive Press campaign in Britain itself, and re-echoed in the United States of America, the purport of the campaign being that we should surrender or lease our ports to Britain for the conduct of the war.

Now, the aim of our Government uniformly has been to try to bring about good relations between the people of this island and the people of the adjoining island. . . . we strove with the British Government to get a complete agreement with regard to all the outstanding issues between us. We succeeded to the extent that with the exception of one outstanding matter, fundamental no doubt, we had settled those outstanding differences in such a way that, if that could only be settled, we could say that the quarrel of the centuries had been ended.

Unfortunately, that outstanding matter, the matter of Partition, which affects so deeply every man and every woman of Irish blood throughout the world, was left unsettled, and it remained unsettled at the outset of this war. But we had settled the points of difference so far as the immediate territory under the jurisdiction of this Government was concerned, and we had hoped that these matters were settled for ever and that never again was there going to be any question of the right of the people of this part of Ireland to exercise complete sovereignty over this territory and to be able to choose the policy which would best seem to serve the interests of the community that lived in the territory . . . it has been understood and that there has not been since the beginning of this war a single suggestion that this community of ours was not entitled to act as we have acted and to remain out of this war.

It is because I am anxious that that should continue that I am choosing this opportunity to address the House and to speak to our people and to the people of the adjoining island. We have chosen the policy of neutrality in this war because we believed that it was the right policy for our people. It is the policy which has been accepted, not merely by this House, but by our people as a whole, and nobody who realises what modern war means, and what it means particularly for those who have not sufficient air defences, will have the slightest doubt that that policy was the right one, apart altogether from any questions of sympathy on one side or the other.

We want friendly relations with the people of Britain. . . . It was partly for that reason, and partly because I knew perfectly that it was a condition of neutrality, that, years before we came into office and several times since we came into office, I announced that it would be our policy to use our strength to the utmost to see that this island was not going to be used as a basis of attack upon Britain. We have never swerved in the slightest from that declaration. Everything that we could do has been done to make sure that that policy would be made as effective as it was within our power to make it. . . .

It is a lie to say that German submarines or any other submarines are being supplied with fuel or provisions on our coasts. A most extensive system of coast observation has been established here since the war. I say it is a lie, and I say further that it is known to be a falsehood by the British Government itself.

Having said all that, I now come to the question of the handing over of these ports so long as this State remains neutral. There can be no question of leasing these ports. They are ours. They are within our sovereignty, and there can be no question, as long as we remain neutral, of handing them over on any condition whatsoever. Any attempt to bring pressure to bear on us by any side—by any of the belligerents—by Britain—could only lead to bloodshed.

Certainly, as long as this Government remains in office, we shall defend our rights in regard to these ports against whoever shall attack them, as we shall defend our rights in regard to every other part of our territory. . . .

I want to say to our people that we may be—I hope not—facing a grave crisis. If we are to face it, then we shall do it, anyhow, knowing that our cause is right and just and that, if we have to die for it, we shall be dying in that good cause.

40

"Bloody Sunday" (January 30, 1972)

The shooting of civilians by British paratroopers opened a more violent phase of the Northern Ireland struggle, although the campaign of the Irish Republican Army had already commenced. This is from the report of Simon Winchester in the independent newspaper, *The Guardian*, January 31, 1972. *Source*: O'Day and Stevenson, 225-26. Copyright *The Guardian*.

The tragic and inevitable Doomsday situation which had been universally forecast for Northern Ireland arrived in Londonderry yesterday afternoon when soldiers, firing into a large crowd of civil rights demonstrators, shot and killed 13 civilians.

Fifteen more people, including a woman, were wounded by gunfire and another woman was seriously injured after being knocked down by an armoured car. The army reported two military casualties and said that its soldiers had arrested between 50 and 60 people who had been allegedly involved in the illegal protest march.

After the shooting, which lasted for about 25 minutes in and around the Rossville Flats area of Bogside, the streets had all the appearance of the aftermath of Sharpeville. Where only moments before, thousands of men and women had been milling around drifting slowly towards a protest meeting to be held at Free Derry Corner, there was a handful of bleeding bodies, some lying still, others still moving with pain, on the white concrete of the square.

The army's official explanation for the killing was that their troops had fired in response to a number of snipers who had opened up on them from below the flats. But those of us at the meeting heard only one shot before the soldiers opened up with their high-velocity rifles.

And, while it is impossible to be absolutely sure, one came away with the firm impression, reinforced by dozens of eye witnesses that the soldiers, men of the 1st Battalion the Parachute Regiment, flown in specifically from Belfast, may have fired needlessly into the huge crowd. . . .

41

The Anglo-Irish Agreement, 1985

The Hillsborough agreement, negotiated between Prime Minister Margaret Thatcher and Taoiseach Garret Fitzgerald, and signed on November 15, 1985, provided the framework for all subsequent peace negotiations among the parties in Northern Ireland.

Source: British Information Services news release, November 15, 1985; editor's copy.

Agreement between the Government of the United Kingdom of Great Britain and Northern Ireland and the Government of the Republic of Ireland.

The Government of the United Kingdom of Great Britain and Northen Ireland and the government of the Republic of Ireland:

wishing further to develop the unique relationship between their peoples and the close co-operation between their countries as friendly neighbours and as partners in the European Community:

recognising the major interest of both their countries and, above all, of the people of Northern Ireland in diminishing the divisions there and achieving lasting peace and stability;

recognising the need for continuing efforts to reconcile and to acknowledge the rights of the two major traditions that exist in Ireland, represented on the one hand by those who wish for no change in the present status of Northern Ireland and on the other hand by those who aspire to a sovereign united Ireland achieved by peaceful means and through agreement;

reaffirming their total rejection of any attempt to promote political objectives by violence or the threat of violence and their determination to work together to ensure that those who adopt or support such methods do not succeed;

recognising that a condition of genuine reconciliation and dialogue between Unionists and Nationalists is mutual recognition and acceptance of each other's rights;

recognising and respecting the identities of the two communities in Northern Ireland, and the right of each to pursue its aspirations by peaceful and constitutional means;

reaffirming their commitment to a society in Northern Ireland in which all may live in peace, free from discrimination and intolerance, and with the opportunity for both communities to participate fully in the structures and processes of government;

have accordingly agreed as follows:

A. Status of Northern Ireland

Article 1

The two Governments
(a) affirm that any change in the status of Northern Ireland would only come about with the consent of a majority of the people of Northern Ireland;
(b) recognise that the present wish of a majority of the people

of Northern Ireland is for no change in the status of Northern Ireland;

(c) declare that, if in the future a majority of the people of Northern Ireland clearly wish for and formally consent to the establishment of a united Ireland, they will introduce and support in the respective Parliaments legislation to give effect to that wish.

B. The Intergovernmental Conference

Article 2

(a) There is hereby established, within the framework of the Anglo-Irish Intergovernmental Council set up after the meeting between the two Heads of Government on 6 November 1981, an Intergovernmental Conference (hereinafter referred to as 'the Conference'), concerned with Northern Ireland and with relations between the two parts of the island of Ireland, to deal, as set out in this Agreement, on a regular basis with

    (i) political matters;

    (ii) security and related matters;

    (iii) legal matters, including the administration of justice;

    (iv) the promotion of cross-border co-operation.

(b) The United Kingdom Government accept that the Irish Government will put forward views and proposals on matters relating to Northern Ireland within the field of activity of the Conference insofar as those matters are not the responsibility of a devolved administration in Northen Ireland. In the interest of promoting peace and stability, determined efforts shall be made through the Conference to resolve any differences. The Conference will be mainly concerned with

Northern Ireland; but some of the matters under consideration will involve co-operative action in both parts of the island of Ireland, and possibly also in Great Britain. Some of the proposals considered in respect of Northern Ireland may also be found to have application by the Irish Government. There is no derogation from the sovereignty of either the United Kingdom Government or the Irish Government, and each retains responsibility for the decisions and administration of government within its own jurisdiction.

Article 3

The Conference shall meet at Ministerial or official level, as required. The business of the Conference will thus receive attention at the highest level. Regular and frequent Ministerial meetings shall be held; and in particular special meetings shall be convened at the request of either side. Officials may meet in subordinate groups. Membership of the Conference and of sub-groups shall be small and flexible. When the Conference meets at Ministerial level the Secretary of State for Northern Ireland and an Irish Minister designated as the Permanent Irish Ministerial Representative shall be joint Chairmen. Within the framework of the Conference other British and Irish Ministers may hold or attend meetings as appropriate; when legal matters are under consideration the Attorneys General may attend. Ministers may be accompanied by their official and their professional advisers: for example, when questions of security policy or security co-operation are being discussed, they may be accompanied by the Chief Constable of the Royal Ulster Constabulary and the Commissioner of the Garda Síochána; or when questions of economic or social policy or co-operation are being discussed, they may be accompanied by officials of the relevant departments. A Secretariat shall be established by the two Governments to service the Conference on a continuing basis in the discharge of its functions as set out in this Agreement.

Article 4

(a) In relation to matters coming within its field of activity, the Conference shall be a framework within which the United Kingdom Government and the Irish Government work together

    (i) for the accommodation of the rights and identities of the two traditions which exist in Northern Ireland; and

    (ii) for peace, stability and prosperity throughout the island of Ireland by promoting reconciliation, respect for human rights, co-operation against terrorism and the development of economic, social and cultural co-operation.

(b) It is the declared policy of the United Kingdom Government that responsibility in respect of certain matters within the powers of the Secretary of State for Northern Ireland should be devolved within Northern Ireland on a basis which would secure widespread acceptance throughout the community. The Irish Government support that policy.

(c) Both Governments recognise that devolution can be achieved only with the co-operation of constitutional representatives within Northern Ireland of both traditions there. The Conference shall be a framework within which the Irish Government may put forward views and proposals on the modalities of bringing about devolution in Northern Ireland, in so far as they relate to the interests of the minority community.

Article 5

(a) The Conference shall concern itself with measures to recognise and accommodate the rights and identities of the two traditions in Northern Ireland, to protect human rights and to prevent discrimination. Matters to be considered in this area include measures to foster the cultural heritage of both traditions, changes in electoral arrangements, the use of flags and emblems, the avoidance of economic and social discrimination and the advantages and disadvantages of a Bill of Rights in some form in Northern Ireland.

(b) The discussion of these matters shall be mainly concerned with Northern Ireland, but the possible application of any measures pursuant to this Article by the Irish Government in their jurisdiction shall not be excluded.

(c) If it should prove impossible to achieve and sustain devolution on a basis which secures widespread acceptance in Northen Ireland, the Conference shall be a framework within which the Irish Government may, where the interests of the minority community are significantly or especially affected, put forward views on proposals for major legislation and on major policy issues, which are within the purview of the Northen Ireland Departments and which remain the responsibility of the Secretary of State for Northern Ireland. . .

D. Security and Related Matters

Article 7

(a) The Conference shall consider
    (i) security policy;

(ii) relations between the security forces and the community;

(iii) prisons policy.

(b) The Conference shall consider the security situation at its regular meetings and thus provide an opportunity to address policy issues, serious incidents and forthcoming events.

(c) The two Governments agree that there is a need for a programme of special measures in Northern Ireland to improve relations between the security forces and the community, with the object in particular of making the security forces more readily accepted by the nationalist community. Such a programme shall be developed, for the Conference's consideration, and may include the establishment of local consultative machinery, training in community relations, crime prevention schemes involving the community, improvements in arrangements for handling complaints, and action to increase the proportion of members of the minority in the Royal Ulster Constabulary. Elements of the programme may be considered by the Irish Government suitable for application within their jurisdiction.

(d) The Conference may consider policy issues relating to prisons. Individual cases may be raised as appropriate, so that information can be provided or inquiries instituted.

E. Legal Matters, Including the Administration of Justice

Article 8

The Conference shall deal with issues of concern to both countries relating to the enforcement of the criminal law. In particular it shall consider whether there are areas of the criminal law applying in the North and in the South respectively which might with benefit be harmonised. The two Governments agree on the importance of public confidence in the administration of justice. The Conference shall seek, with the help of advice from experts as appropriate, measures which would give substantial expression to this aim, considering inter alia the possibility of mixed courts in both jurisdictions for the trial of certain offences. The Conference shall also be concerned with policy aspects of extradition and extraterritorial jurisdiction as between North and South.

F. Cross-Border Co-operation on Security, Economic, Social and Cultural Matters

Article 9

(a) With a view to enhancing cross-border co-operation on security matters, the Conference shall set in hand a programme of work to be undertaken by the Chief Constable of the Royal Ulster Constabulary and the Commissioner of the Garda Síochána and, where appropriate, groups of officials, in such areas as threat assessments, exchange of information, liaison structures, technical co-operation, training of personnel, and operational resources.

(b) The Conference shall have no operational responsibilities; responsibility for police operations shall remain with the heads of the respective police forces, the Chief Constable of the Royal Ulster Constabulary maintaining his links with the Secretary of State for Northen Ireland and the Commissioner of the Garda Síochána his links with the Minister of Justice.

Article 10

(a) The two Governments shall co-operate to promote the economic and social development of those areas of both parts of Ireland which have suffered most severely from the consequences of the instability of recent years, and shall consider the possibility of securing international support for this work.

(b) If it should prove impossible to achieve and sustain devolution on a basis which secures widespread acceptance in Northen Ireland, the Conference shall be a framework for the promotion of co-operation between the two parts of Ireland concerning cross-border aspects of economic, social and cultural matters in relation to which the Secretary of State for Northern Ireland continues to exercise authority. .

42

The Agreement (1998)

This multi-party agreement (sometimes called the Good Friday agreement, or the Belfast agreement) was signed by all the participants in the Belfast negotiations on April 10, 1998, with the assent of the British and Irish governments. The first section printed here is the opening portion of the agreement among the Northen Ireland parties; the second section is the agreement of the governments, a proper treaty. The Northern Irish parties implemented the Agreement in November 1999.

Source: British Information Services Press Release, Friday, 10 April 1998; editor's copy.

1. We, the participants in the multi-party negotiations, believe that the agreement we have negotiated offers a truly historic opportunity for a new beginning.

2. The tragedies of the past have left a deep and profoundly regrettable legacy of suffering.

We must never forget those who have died or been injured, and their families. But we can best honour them through a fresh start, in which we firmly dedicate ourselves to the achievement of reconciliation, tolerance, and mutual trust, and to the protection and vindication of the human rights of all.

3. We are committed to partnership, equality and mutual respect as the basis of relationships within Northern Ireland, be-

tween North and South, and between these islands.

4. We reaffirm our total and absolute commitment to exclusively democratic and peaceful means of resolving differences on political issues, and our opposition to any use or threat of force by others for any political purpose, whether in regard to this agreement or otherwise.

5. We acknowledge the substantial differences between our continuing, and equally legitimate, political aspirations. However, we will endeavour to strive in every practical way towards reconciliation and rapprochement within the framework of democratic and agreed arrangements. We pledge that we will, in good faith, work to ensure the success of each and every one of the arrangements to be established under this agreement. It is accepted that all of the institutional and constitutional arrangements—an Assembly in Northern Ireland, a North/South Ministerial Council, implementation bodies, a British-Irish Council and a British-Irish Intergovernmental Conference and any amendments to British Acts of Parliament and the Constitution of Ireland—are interlocking and interdependent and that in particular the functioning of the Assembly and the North/South Council are so closely inter-related that the success of each depends on that of the other.

6. Accordingly, in a spirit of concord, we strongly commend this agreement to the people, North and South, for their approval.

Constitutional Issues

1. The participants endorse the commitment made by the British and Irish Governments that, in a new British-Irish Agreement replacing the Anglo-Irish Agreement, they will:

  (ii) recognise the legitimacy of whatever choice is freely exercised by a majority of the people of Northern

Ireland with regard to its status, whether they prefer to continue to support the Union with Great Britain or a sovereign united Ireland;

(iii) recognise that it is for the people of the island of Ireland alone, by agreement between the two parts respectively and without external impediment, to exercise their right of self-determination on the basis of consent, freely and concurrently given, North and South, to bring about a united Ireland, if that is their wish, accepting that this right must be achieved and exercised with and subject to the agreement and consent of a majority of the people of Northern Ireland;

(iv) acknowledge that while a substantial section of the people in Northen Ireland share the legitimate wish of a majority of the people of the island of Ireland for a united Ireland, the present wish of a majority of the people of Northern Ireland, freely exercised and legitimate, is to maintain the Union and, accordingly, that Northen Ireland's status as part of the United Kingdom reflects and relies upon that wish; and that it would be wrong to make any change in the status of Northern Ireland save with the consent of a majority of its people;

(v) affirm that if, in the future, the people of the island of Ireland exercise their right of self-determination on the basis set out in sections (i) and (ii) above to bring about a united Ireland, it will be a binding obligation on both Governments to introduce and support in their respective Parliaments legislation to give effect to that wish;

(vi) affirm that whatever choice is freely exercised by a majority of the people of Northern Ireland, the power of the sovereign government with jurisdiction there shall be exercised with rigorous impartiality on behalf of all the people in the diversity of their identities and traditions and shall be founded on the principles of full respect for, and equality of, civil, political, social and cultural rights, of freedom from discrimination for all citizens, and of parity of esteem and of just and equal treatment for the identity, ethos, and aspirations of both communities;

(vii) recognise the birthright of all the people of Northern Ireland to identify themselves and be accepted as Irish or British, or both, as they may so choose, and accordingly confirm that their right to hold both British and Irish citizenship is accepted by both Governments and would not be affected by any future change in the status of Northen Ireland.

2. The participants also note that the two Governments have accordingly undertaken in the context of this comprehensive political agreement, to propose and support changes in, respectively, the Constitution of Ireland and in British legislation relating to the constitutional status of Northern Ireland.

The British and Irish Governments:

Welcoming the strong commitment to the Agreement reached on 10th April 1998 by themselves and other participants in the multi-party talks and set out in Annex 1 to this Agreement (hereinafter the Multi-Party Agreement)

Considering that the Multi-Party Agreement offers an opportunity for a new beginning in relationships within Northern Ireland, within the island of Ireland and between the peoples of these islands;

Wishing to develop still further the unique relationship between their peoples and the close co-operation between their countries as friendly neighbours and as partners in the European Union;

Reaffirming their total commitment to the principles of democracy and non-violence which have been fundamental to the multi-party talks;

Reaffirming their commitment to the principles of partnership, equality and mutual respect and to the protection of civil, political, social, economic and cultural rights in their respective jurisdictions;

Have agreed as follows:

Article 1

The two Governments:

    (i) recognise the legitimacy of whatever choice is freely exercised by a majority of the people of Northern Ireland with regard to its status, whether they prefer to continue to support the Union with Great Britain or a sovereign united Ireland;

    (ii) recognise that it is for the people of the island of Ireland alone, by agreement between the two parts respectively and without external impediment, to exercise their right of self-determination on the basis of consent, freely and concurrently given, North and South, to bring about a united Ireland, if that is their wish, accepting that this right must be achieved and exercised with and subject to the agreement and consent of a majority of the people of Northern Ireland;

    (iii) acknowledge that while a substantial section of the

people in Northern Ireland share the legitimate wish of a majority of the people of the island of Ireland for a united Ireland, the present wish of a majority of the people of Northern Ireland, freely exercised and legitimate, is to maintain the Union and accordingly, that Northern Ireland's status as part of the United Kingdom reflects and relies upon that wish; and that it would be wrong to make any change in the status of Northern Ireland save with the consent of a majority of its people;

(iv) affirm that, if in the future, the people of the island of Ireland exercise their right of self-determination on the basis set out in sections (i) and (ii) above to bring about a united Ireland, it will be a binding obligation on both Governments to introduce and support in their respective Parliaments legislation to give effect to that wish;

(v) affirm that whatever choice is freely exercised by a majority of the people of Northern Ireland, the power of the sovereign government with jurisdiction there shall be exercised with rigorous impartiality on behalf of all the people in the diversity of their identities and traditions and shall be founded on the principles of full respect for, and equality of, civil, political, social and cultural rights, of freedom from discrimination for all citizens, and of parity of esteem and of just and equal treatment for the identity, ethos and aspirations of both communities;

(vi) recognise the birthright of all the people of Northern Ireland to identify themselves and be accepted as Irish or British, or both, as they may so choose, and accordingly confirm that their right to hold both

150

British and Irish citizenship is accepted by both Governments and would not be affected by any future change in the status of Northern Ireland.

Article 2

The two Governments affirm their solemn commitment to support, and where appropriate implement, the provisions of the Multi-Party Agreement. In particular there shall be established in accordance with the provisions of the Multi-Party Agreement immediately on the entry into force of this Agreement, the following institutions:

   (i) a North/South Ministerial Council;

   (ii) the implementation bodies referred to in paragraph 9 (ii) of the section entitled "Strand Two" of the Multi-Party Agreement;

   (iii) a British-Irish Council;

   (iv) a British-Irish Intergovernmental Conference . . . .

About the Editor

Josef L. Altholz received his Ph.D. from Columbia University in 1960 and has taught at the University of Minnesota since 1959. His field is the history of the British Isles, chiefly religious, in modern times; he has taught Irish history since 1979. His books include *The Liberal Catholic Movement in England, The Churches in the Nineteenth Century, The Religious Press in Britain*, and *Anatomy of a Controversy*.